Assessing
Organizational
Effectiveness

SUNY Series on Administrative Systems
Mariann Jelinek
Editor

Assessing Organizational Effectiveness

Systems Change, Adaptation, and Strategy

Raymond F. Zammuto

National Center for
Higher Education Management Systems

State University of New York Press
Albany

Published by
State University of New York Press, Albany

© 1982 State University of New York

For information, address State University of New York
Press, State University Plaza, Albany, N.Y., 12246

Library of Congress Catalog in Publication Data

Zammuto, Raymond F.
    Assessing organizational effectiveness.

    (SUNY Press series on administrative systems)
    Includes bibliographical references.
    1. Organizational effectiveness. I. Title.
II. Series.
HD58.9.Z35   658.4'01   81-9130
ISBN 0-87395-552-8   AACR2
ISBN 0-87395-553-6 (pbk.)

Table 1.2. is reprinted by permission of the
publisher, from *Management Review,* March 1978
© 1978 by AMACOM, a division of American Management
Associations, p. 10. All rights reserved.

Contents

Tables

Figures

Preface

This book proposes an evolutionary model for judging the performance of organizations and explores how these judgments are related to the continued viability of organizations and society as a whole. The impetus for writing it was the result of an evolution of my own.

The origins of these ideas can be traced back to my involvement in advocating a particular point of view concerning social reform. I became interested in why people judged the same situation differently. The logic of their judgments, based on their stake in the situation, was impeccable. This raised the dilemma of "who was right and who was wrong?" While struggling with this dilemma, I assumed the role of a program evaluator for a nurse practitioner program. The qualitative data from the program evaluations indicated that it was often the context in which performance occurred, rather than performance per se, that determined effectiveness.

Later, I put on the hat of a policy analyst studying the impact of federal and state policies on age discrimination in employment. During the process of trying to trace out the effects of these policies, the glimmering of an evolutionary perspective began to emerge. A first attempt at integrating these ideas was made in the form of my doctoral thesis at the University of Illinois, Urbana. The ideas were refined at Wayne State University in Detroit where I was teaching courses about the relationship between business and society, or, as I referred to them, courses on "applied organization theory." While in Detroit, I had the opportunity to witness the auto industry go through a wrenching period of change. I also had the opportunity to talk with auto company managers and executives who were trying to cope with the situation. All these experiences contributed to the evolution of the ideas within.

While this book advocates an evolutionary perspective on organizational effectiveness, it should be read within the context of it being only one of many possible explanations which exist in the literature. A number of different perspectives are discussed in Chapter 2, all of which offer insight into the concept. The book's purpose is to stimulate ideas and discussion—to make people think—not to proclaim the "truth." My time will have been well spent if it accomplishes this end.

Writing a manuscript can be achieved only with the help and forbearance of one's friends and colleagues. I am grateful to many individuals: to Lou Pondy, Mike Moch, and Hugh Petrie for their support and stimulation while this was being written as a dissertation; to Dan Alpert, Peggy Harris, and the Center for Advanced Study for providing encouragement and a home away from home; to Terry Connolly, Mariann Jelinek, Marilyn Israel, and Kim Cameron for their comments on later drafts; and to the auto industry executives who shared their own experiences with me in preparation for the case study presented in Chapter 5. I would especially like to thank Nate Borofsky for his thoughtful comments and editing, and my wife Marilyn for putting up with and supporting this effort over the years. Adrianne Stach and Sue Ristovski cheerfully performed most of the tasks associated with producing the manuscript. Finally, I would like to dedicate this book to my parents, who did not have an opportunity to see it in print. They would have been kind enough to have been proud of the effort.

1

Performance and Legitimacy

This is a book about the everyday human activity of judging the effectiveness of organizational performance. Judging effectiveness is something that everyone does on a continuous, ongoing basis. Every individual evaluates the performance of organizations based on how they affect that person. Take a common everyday activity like banking. When I moved to Detroit I opened an account at the Next-to-Last National Bank of Detroit (NLNBD). The first few times that I went to NLNBD to cash a check or make a deposit I had to wait in line for half an hour. Since waiting in line for half an hour is personally undesirable, I judged NLNBD to be performing ineffectively. My neighbor, who also does his banking at NLNBD, likes the bank because it has friendly tellers. His preferences for banking run along the line of personalized service, of which friendly tellers are a part. He considers waiting in line simply to be a reasonable cost of doing business with a bank offering personalized service. To him, NLNBD performs effectively.

These judgments are remarkably accurate and relatively uncomplicated because each person is the final arbiter in deciding whether something is personally desirable. They also play an important role in our lives because judgments of effectiveness influence the nature of relationships people will have with organizations. If individuals believe an organization is performing effectively, they are likely to continue dealing with it. In performing effectively, the organization is having personally desirable effects on an individual. The relationship is, in other words, producing desirable outcomes. If a relationship with an organization is unsatisfactory in the sense that it is producing personally undesirable outcomes, individuals will terminate it, particularly if alternatives are available.

Since I had to wait in line at NLNBD all the time, I decided to change banks. Given my idiosyncratic preferences, I moved my banking business to the Last National Bank of Detroit (LNBD), which offered twenty-four hour banking services via machine. After a year's experience with LNBD, I have come to consider it an effective organization. I never have to wait in line and even conduct my banking during the middle of the night. My neighbor wouldn't even consider LNBD as an option since he dislikes machines. They aren't friendly and they depersonalize the services rendered. The point is that people evaluate the effectiveness of organizational performance based on their experience with organizations and the impact of organizational performance on them in light of their preferences. These individual evaluations are relatively straightforward since they are based on our own preferences and are used to guide our own actions.

Judgments of organizational effectiveness are considerably more complex than individual judgments of performance. The concept of organizational effectiveness implies that a judgment on the effectiveness of an organization's overall performance is being rendered. Every organization has many constituencies, each of whom judges effectiveness from its own idiosyncratic perspective. All these constituencies provide valid information about organizational performance because they are affected by it. Part of the difficulty arises when the question of whose perspective of performance is to be used in reaching a judgment of organizational effectiveness. Not all dimensions of organizational performance are taken into account by constituencies in making their judgments. Only those specific facets of performance which are important to individuals enter into their assessments. Hence, different constituencies evaluate different aspects of an organization's total performance.

In the case of the Next-to-Last National Bank of Detroit, I judged the organization as performing ineffectively because I had to wait in line to conduct my transactions. Waiting in line is a very minute aspect of the bank's total performance. Although it is only a small part of performance, it was personally important because it affected me. Shareholders, on the other hand, might judge the bank as performing effectively because it provides a good return on their investment, something which is important to them. They couldn't care less about my waiting in line nor I about their return on investment. Employees may judge NLNBD as performing ineffectively because it pays relatively low wages and has archaic personnel policies. Suppliers of the bank might judge it as performing effectively because it provides a steady source of business and pays its bills promptly. Community groups might assess NLNBD as performing ineffectively because they have uncovered evidence that it is red-lining local neighborhoods. Each constituency of an organization provides a different window through which performance can be viewed, but none of the constituencies judge all aspects of an organization's performance.

Judgments of organizational effectiveness serve an important social function in that they guide social behavior in much the same way that individual judgments of performance guide individual behavior. Organizational effectiveness reflects the degree to which an organization is being responsive to constituent preferences for performance. If an organization is performing effectively, it is meeting the demands of its constituencies in terms of what they define as desirable outcomes of performance. If an organization is not satisfying constituent preferences for performance, constituents will search for alternative sources to satisfy their preferences. If alternatives are not available, constituents will create pressures within the larger social arena for the creation of alternatives. In either case, the long-term survival of the ineffective organization is jeopardized.

Another factor which adds complexity to the concept of organizational effectiveness is that constituent preferences for performance change over time. As preferences for performance change, the actual criteria or the way in which constituencies employ existing criteria in evaluating organizational performance change. An unusually dramatic example of this was the shift in the consuming public's demand for automotive products during the 1970s. The American auto industry had performed effectively in terms of the consumers' preference for large luxury automobiles for many years. But, public preferences for automobiles changed radically during the 1970s. The first marked shift occurred because of the 1973-4 OPEC oil embargo; the second as gas prices rose dramatically in 1979. Both situations created uncertainty over the continued price and supply of gasoline, which resulted in consumer preferences shifting markedly toward small-size automobiles. Since the American auto industry was perceived as being unable to satisfy these new preferences, many Americans bought cars produced by foreign automakers. The impact of shifting preferences on the American auto companies was indisputable. Their long-term viability was severely jeopardized because changes in their performance did not keep pace with changing consumer preferences.

Cast into this type of framework, discussion of the nature and assessment of organizational effectiveness raises a set of questions somewhat different from those typically encountered. Such discussions often raise questions concerning the attainment of managerially preordained goals in that effective performance is usually defined as that which creates managerially desired effects. Within this framework, questions are raised about the degree to which an organization is satisfying broad sets of preferences for performance, as defined by the organization's constituencies. Satisfaction of constituent preferences is important because it is a requirement of their continued participation in the organization. Indeed, effective organizations thrive because of the active participation of their constituencies.

It is useful to remember that organizations are social inventions created to satisfy human needs. As Coleman (1974) noted, the corporate form, or juristic person in law, evolved to satisfy social needs that were difficult or impossible to satisfy via individual action. Although this form of activity evolved to attain ends which could not be achieved individually, organizations can attain these ends only through individual action. They have no innate ability to act. Organizations act only through their human agents. The term agent is not limited to those persons who are usually considered to fall within the boundaries of the organization, but refers to all organizational participants. This includes customers, suppliers, creditors, and so on, as well as employers, managers, and shareholders. All these individuals are party to the nexus of human interaction within society that is the organization. They participate in exchange relationships with the organization because it provides self-defined valued outcomes. Continued participation is dependent on the continued creation by the organization of valued outcomes as defined by the participants. Organizations gain their license to exist by creating these valued outcomes. It is through the satisfaction of the wants and needs of members of society that society in turn legitimizes an organization's existence.

This characterization of organizational effectiveness transforms the concept in two important ways. First, tying the concept of organization effectiveness together with the notion of social legitimacy exposes the underlying reason why it is an important construct. Organizations have to perform effectively in order to survive. Effective organizations, evolving in tandem with the larger society, modify their performance to meet changing social needs and constraints. Second, it gives the concept a greater degree of reality. Managers deal with changing constituent preferences on a day-to-day basis. The environment in which managers operate is dynamic. Current models of organizational effectiveness treat preferences as if they were static. As a result, managers often find theoretically based evaluations of performance rather sterile, providing little information useful for decision making. The model presented in Chapter 3 reconciles the divergence between the theory and practice of evaluation research and organizational effectiveness.

Social legitimacy and changing constituent preferences for performance are important aspects of today's managerial environment. Survey results indicate that the public doesn't believe that the performance of various institutions is creating socially desirable outcomes. These institutions are being judged as performing ineffectively. The organizations which make up these institutions are facing a crisis of legitimacy which jeopardizes their survival. The following examines this crisis and the relationship of changing expectations with actual institutional performance.

Public Confidence in Societal Institutions

One measure of overall effectiveness of societal institutions, those populations of organizations which comprise the infrastructure of society, is the degree to which the public has confidence in them. It is plausible to assume that if institutions are producing desirable outcomes, the public will have confidence in them. If they are not performing effectively from the perspective of the public, confidence in institutions and institutional leadership will decline.

Louis Harris and Associates have been polling the American public since 1966 about their confidence in institutional leadership. Periodically, a national sample has been asked, "How much confidence do you have in the leadership of (name of a major institution)?" The results of the polls, presented in Table 1-1, show a substantial decline in public confidence in institutional leadership from 1966 to 1978. In 1966, at least 50 percent of the public expressed a great deal of confidence in the leadership of five out of twelve societal institutions. The average level of confidence in the twelve institutions was 44 percent, with medicine receiving the highest rating (73 percent) and advertising the lowest (21 percent). By 1978, none of the fourteen institutions included in the poll received a rating of a great deal of confidence by the majority of the public. In fact, the average rating of 23 percent was only marginally higher than that of the lowest rated institution in 1966.

The decline in public confidence is serious because it reflects a decline in the viability of society as a whole. As public confidence decreases, social institutions lose the basis of their legitimacy, which is the first step toward social decline. Society begins to unravel. As Boulding (1978: 205-6) observed:

Legitimacy does come from positive payoffs in the sense of institutions or individuals that create satisfactions. It is perhaps seen most clearly when institutions, which have previously paid off, no longer do and then they often

Table 1-1. Public Confidence in the Leadership of Major Social Institutions

Institution	Percent having a great deal of confidence in the leadership of:							
	1966	1972	1973	1974	1975	1976	1977	1978
Congress	42	21	29	18	13	9	17	10
Supreme Court	50	28	33	40	28	22	29	29
Federal Gov't. (Exec)	41	27	19	28	13	11	23	14
State Government	NA	NA	24	NA	NA	16	18	15
Local Government	NA	NA	28	NA	NA	21	18	19
The Press	29	18	30	25	26	20	18	23
TV News	25	17	41	31	35	28	28	35
Higher Education	61	33	44	40	36	31	37	41
Organized Religion	41	30	36	32	32	24	29	34
Major Companies	55	27	29	21	19	16	20	22
Organized Labor	27	15	20	18	14	10	14	15
Law Firms	NA	NA	24	18	16	12	14	18
Advertising	21	NA	11	NA	7	7	7	11
Medicine	73	48	57	50	43	42	43	42
Military	62	35	40	33	24	23	27	NA

SOURCE: Lou Harris and Associates.

tend to lose legitimacy even though the inertia of the system may keep them going for quite a while. . . . Institutions that seem absolutely unshakable today may be in ruins next year when the system goes over an unforeseen precipice.

Ineffective performance threatens the survival of both the institutions and the larger society.

Declines in confidence occur because of an increasing divergence between what the public wants from social institutions and what they deliver in terms of performance. The relationship between the demands for performance and actual performance is displayed graphically in Figure 1-1. The horizontal axis represents a unit of time while the vertical axis is some measure of quantity-quality. The upper curve represents the public's expectations for performance, while the lower curve is the actual level of institutional performance. The area between the two curves can be viewed as the "social anxiety factor." Social anxiety increases as the distance between expectations for performance and actual performance increases. In short, confidence in institutions declines because they are not meeting public demands for performance.

Performance expectations can change quantitatively and qualitatively. Quantitatively, individuals may demand "more, bigger, and better" of the same types of performance that the institutions have delivered in the past. As people become used to what they have, they often desire and strive to obtain more of the same. The public, for example, has always demanded a higher material standard of living, a demand which societal institutions have for the most part met.

Qualitative changes in preferences for performance present a more difficult challenge to institutions. Such changes involve basic shifts in what the public considers to be desirable. The history of the 1960s and 1970s is illustrative. The public became interested, for the first time, in a number of new concerns. It began demanding improvements in environmental quality, increased participation in institutional decision making, equality of opportunity for all members of society, and so on. These demands were symptomatic of basic shifts in public preferences.

It is important to emphasize that the "social anxiety factor" is a function of the relationship between public demands for performance and actual institutional performance. Examining changes in preferences alone is insufficient to gain an understanding of the dynamics involved. It is also important to note that the institutional perception of and response to quantitative and qualitative changes are often different. Generally, social institutions have been perceptive of and responsive to quantitative changes in demands for performance. This type of change

Figure I–I

The Relationship Between Public Expectations for and Actual Institutional Performance

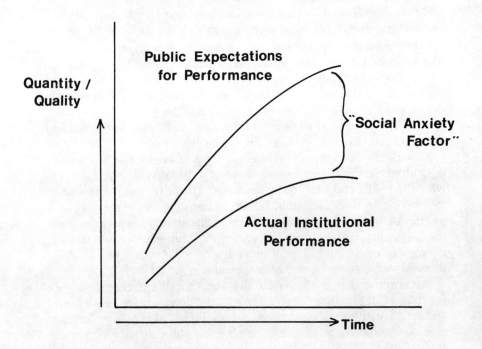

in public expectations is often closely aligned with the interests of the institutions themselves. Major companies, for example, are responsive to quantitative changes in expectations because they represent changes in the demand for the goods and services of business. Responding to such changes usually requires quantitative adjustments or modifications in current organizational performance. Qualitative change, on the other hand, represents basic deviations from previous expectations. This often involves movement away from a previous set of expectations rather than movement toward a new set of expectations, making the eventual end point of qualitative changes problematic. Such expectations require that institutions *do something differently* instead of doing more of the same thing.

Given the nature of institutional control mechanisms, quantitative changes in expectations for performance are relatively easy to detect since institutional managers are trained to look for them. On the level of an individual organization, this means observing and acting upon changes in the demand for goods and services. Qualitative changes are more difficult to detect because they represent basic changes in the nature of performance that the public is expecting. The changes are often unexpected and institutional managers don't know what to look for. In many cases, qualitative changes in preferences are not acted upon because institutional managers don't perceive them. Once noticed, changes are often discounted as errors in perception or anomalies because they fall outside the domain of normal managerial experience. Hence, they are not responded to. It is often qualitative changes in public preferences for performance that result in an expansion of the "social anxiety factor" and declining public confidence. The following illustrates the nature of these changes in American society and the responses of a major social institution, business, to them.

American Business and Public Confidence

Traditionally, American business has been one of the most respected institutions in American society. This occurred largely because of a convergence in social, political, moral, and economic philosophies during early U.S. history.[1] American democracy and the notion of individualism fit well with capitalism. Individualism and free choice reinforced the utilitarian underpinnings of capitalism. They all suggested that the greatest social good would result when individuals dili-

---

1. For a detailed analysis, see: Cavanagh, G. C., *American Business Values in Transition*, (Englewood Cliffs, N.J.: Prentice-Hall, 1976).

gently pursued their own self-interest. The tenets of Protestantism also reinforced capitalism. Protestantism, and particularly the teachings of Calvin, held that hard work and thrift were the road to salvation. The accumulation of wealth, pursuant to this Protestant work ethic, was a sign that an individual was one of God's chosen. Capitalism required large amounts of capital and high productivity, both encouraged by Calvinist doctrine. Working hard and accumulating wealth, therefore, were morally, socially, and economically proper. Small wonder that business and businessmen assumed central roles in American society; or, as President Coolidge succinctly noted, "the business of America is business."

This convergence created an environment favorable to rapid industrial development, which resulted in the generation of vast material wealth. By the 1950s, the American public had the highest material standard of living in the world. Paradoxically, it was the very success of the American business system in lifting the majority out of poverty that undermined it. Bell (1976: 74) describes the contradiction this way:

The rising wealth of the plutocracy [in the early 1900s] meant that work and accumulation were no longer ends in themselves, but means of consumption and display. Status and its badges, not work and the election of God, became the marks of success.

By freeing the average individual from the toil required to produce the necessities of life, the very success of the business system weakened the pillars on which it was built. Acquisition and consumption, as Finlay (1977) observed, began to erode the original notions of hard work and thrift.

The success of American business in meeting public preferences was instrumental in changing what the public demanded from it. At first, the public's primary concerns were about physical survival and personal security. It expected business to provide employment and produce the products and services needed for everyday living. As these needs were met for more Americans the U.S. standard of living improved. By the 1950s, however, the national goals of prosperity, material welfare, and economic justice, which had guided corporate and social action, began to be supplanted by a growing concern for environmental quality, improvement in the quality of life, and social justice. Once again, the traditional ideology and goals of the system changed because the system had been successful in meeting its goals.

Davis (1976) explained these changes in public preferences in terms of Maslow's hierarchy of needs. Maslow argued that human needs exist in some order of priority. As basic needs are satisfied, other higher-order needs arise to dominate human expectations. In Maslow's hierarchy, the most basic needs are those dealing with physical survival and personal security, followed by higher-order needs, which are socially-oriented. Since Western industrialized nations have reached a level of development in which most of the basic needs of their citizens have been met, the logic of the model suggests that higher-order, socially-oriented needs would emerge to guide public preferences. The actual emergence of such socially-oriented needs or goals represents a fundamental change in the nature of the expectations for the performance of American social institutions.

It is not difficult to translate these emerging "needs" into concrete changes in public expectations for business performance. Consider the rise of environmentalism in the United States. Throughout the majority of this century belching smokestacks were considered to be a sign of industrial progress, which translated into a higher material standard of living. Air quality in most urban areas of the United States would have been considered unfit for human consumption if judged by today's standards. Bettmann (1974) noted, for example, that Pittsburgh and the surrounding Monongahela Valley had over 14,000 smokestacks at the turn of the century, primarily from the iron and steel plants in the area. A Hungarian visitor to the city at that time described the air as "a noisome vomit, killing everything that grows—trees, grass, and flowers" (Bettmann, 1974: 16). Stagnant weather conditions often aggravated the situation. It was not uncommon for the street lights of Pittsburgh to be turned on in the early afternoon because of the density of the pollutants in the air.

These conditions were not unusual in urban areas at the turn of the century. Even though the air quality was considerably poorer than it is today, the public showed little concern. In fact, the people of Pittsburgh pronounced their city as "one of the healthiest in the United States. . . . People work so hard here they don't notice the smoke" (Bettmann, 1974: 16). Although groups such as the Sierra Club had been promoting environmental quality for a number of years, it wasn't until the 1960s that environmental quality became a national concern. The 1963 publication of Rachael Carson's book, *The Silent Spring,* which described the effect of DDT on the Gulf Coast ecosystem, was a triggering event which raised public awareness of the environmental impact of industrial pollution.

Public concern over environmental quality increased substantially, enough to make it a political issue during the 1968 Presidential election. The political debate eventually resulted in the passage of the National Environmental Protection Act of 1970 and the creation of the Environmental Protection Agency. Other legislation enacted through the 1960s and 1970s covered specific aspects of air, water, solid waste, and toxic chemical pollution. Over a twenty year period, environmental concern became a major factor on the national political agenda and was translated into stringent laws governing the discharge and disposal of industrial effluence. The change in public preferences for performance were clear-cut in this case. The public demanded that business institutions minimize pollution created in the process of producing desired goods and services.

As public expectations change and embrace new areas, they become more sophisticated. Evolving preferences usually begin in a general, undifferentiated form (i.e., a general amorphous concern about environmental quality). As time progresses and the public explores the implications of their changing preferences, the preferences tend to become more specific. Environmental concern was initially directed toward air and water quality, for example, which were areas most obviously affected by industrial pollutants. New areas of environmental concern emerged as more attention was focused on environmental quality. During the mid-1970s, for example, two new environmental issues surfaced, fluorocarbon and toxic waste pollution. Both were more subtle forms of pollution. They did not have the same visual impact as air and water pollution, although the potential health effects were substantial. Fluorocarbon and toxic waste pollution were discovered and brought into the public eye because public attention had focused on environmental issues. Public concern created a climate in which such problems could be discovered and publicly discussed.

In the case of fluorocarbon pollution, scientists discovered that fluorocarbons were depleting ozone in the stratosphere, which allowed more radiation to reach the earth's surface. The projected effect of increased exposure was a significant rise in the occurrence of skin cancer in humans. These findings and projections found their way into the popular press during 1974 and immediately provoked grave public concern. Some producers of consumer spray products employing fluorocarbon propellants saw changing public expectations as a marketing opportunity and rapidly converted their products to use non-fluorocarbon propellants. The federal government shortly thereafter enacted legislation banning most uses of fluorocarbons. It is unlikely that the effects of fluorocarbons on the ozone layer would have been studied if environmental quality had not been a major public concern. The results of the studies would not have received as much public attention if the public had not already been sensitized to such problems by earlier exposure to the effects of air and water pollution. While qualitative changes in public preferences begin to emerge in a very general form, they gain in specificity and sophistication over time. Public concern functions as an attention focusing mechanism.

Qualitative changes in public expectations have occurred in a number of areas in addition to that of environmental quality. Since the mid-1960s, corporations have been expected to provide equal employment opportunities for all members of society, conduct operations in an ethical manner, provide the consumer with high quality products at fair prices, protect the health and safety of employees, and so on. As in the area of environmental quality, expectations in these other areas have grown more sophisticated as the public explores and learns about their desires.

With respect to the model presented in Figure 1-1, these changes reflect qualitative shifts in public preferences for business performance while quantitative preferences have remained relatively stable. The public is demanding that business attend to public concerns for environmental protection, the quality of life, and social justice while fulfilling its traditional economic mission. Quantitatively, public preferences remain much the same in that people still want to enjoy a high material standard of living. The fundamental change, however, is that they also want a higher qualitative standard of living. Many past practices which were tolerated, indeed encouraged, in attaining a higher material standard of living are now actively discouraged by law and public opinion.

Corporate Responses to Changing Public Preferences

It is evident that business has not fully met changing public preferences for performance. The Harris poll data in Table 1-1 shows that public confidence in major companies was the fourth highest of all the institutions surveyed in 1966, when 55 percent of the public expressed a great deal of confidence in business leadership. By 1978, the percentage of the public expressing a great deal of confidence in business leadership had dropped to 22 percent, a 60 percent decline. Another way to characterize the decline in confidence is to examine the public's perception of the degree to which business is operating in a manner which serves the public interest. The opinion survey firm of Yankelovich, Skelly, and White conducted polls over a ten year period which provide some valuable insights. The poll asked individuals whether they agreed with the statement, "Business tries to strike a fair balance between profits and the interests of the public." The results of the poll, presented in Table 1-2, show a dramatic decline in the belief that business is acting in the public interest. In 1968, 70 percent of the public agreed that business tried to strike a fair balance between profit and the public interest. By 1977, only 15 percent of the respondents agreed with the same statement.

Table 1-2. Business Tries to Strike a Fair Balance Between Profits and the Interests of the Public

Year	% Agree
1968	70
1969	58
1970	33
1972	32
1973	34
1974	19
1975	19
1976	15
1977	15

SOURCE: Weiss, E. A. "The Future Opinion of Business," *Management Review,* (March, 1978): 10. Reprinted by permission of the publisher, from *Management Review,* March 1978, © 1978 by AMACOM, a division of American Management Associations, p. 10. All rights reserved.

The reaction of many businessmen to the decline of public confidence was expressed in a *Wall Street Journal* poll as follows:

Few heads of large and medium-sized corporations volunteered suggestions about product quality, fair prices or business ethics. For example, only four percent of the chiefs of medium-sized firms recommended concentrating on high-quality production. And only ten percent of the heads of large corporations mentioned a need for business to maintain ethical standards. . . . Heads of large companies said they see the solution in communicating better and "educating" the public about business, suggesting that the basis of the low esteem is *ignorance* (emphasis added) *(Wall Street Journal,* August 21, 1980: 25).

Corporate leaders have acted on these beliefs in designing programs to regain public confidence. They have attempted to combat "economic illiteracy" by sponsoring and funding economic programs, and have tried to communicate better by speaking out on the issues through advocacy advertising. Both approaches warrant close examination.

Millions of dollars have been spent on economic education programs by American corporations over the last decade. These programs encompass all levels of formal education. Corporations have funded efforts to instruct primary and secondary school teachers in free market economics and developed materials for use in their classrooms. Texas A&M's Center for Education and Research in Free Enterprise, for example, has been endowed by a number of corporations including Phillips Petroleum, Pepsico, and Dow Chemical. The Center specializes in economics training for high school teachers. At the university and college level, corporations have funded academic centers for research and teaching and academic chairs of free enterprise. The University of Texas's Institute for Constructive Capitalism, funded by Mobil, Shell Oil, and Tenneco, among others, is a good example of such a center. Its goal is to "construct a modern ethical and philosophical basis for capitalism"[2] from which free enterprise can be defended. Corporations have also been active in funding and organizing Students in Free Enterprise groups on campuses around the country. These groups are primarily oriented toward creating a better image of corporations on college campuses. By the 1978-9 academic year, these groups had been organized at approximately 150 colleges in twenty states with about 8,000 students actively participating.

The implicit assumption behind such efforts is that the public is ignorant about the way free enterprise works. Hence, free enterprise education should increase economic literacy and make the public more sympathetic to business. This is a questionable assumption, since it can be argued that the public is no more economically illiterate today than it was in the 1950s and 1960s, when confidence in business was much higher. Also, it does not appear to be the efficacy of free enterprise that the public is questioning. A Yankelovich survey, conducted in the mid-1970s, revealed that 91 percent of the public did not favor government ownership or control of large corporations, and that more than two-thirds indicated a willingness to make sacrifices in order to preserve the free enterprise system. Over 70 percent of the public recognized that business profits are necessary for growth.

The educational intent of these programs is also questionable. Kristol (1976: 18) argued that the type of economic education programs that corporations are currently funding are more advertising than education. He noted:

Education, properly understood, induces a growing comprehension of abstract ideas and concepts; advertising, properly understood, aims to move people to

2. "Capitalism 101," *Newsweek*, April 30, 1979.

do something definite and unambiguous. Education is always raising questions, advertising is always giving answers. They are two radically different modes of communication and their admixture is corrupting to both. It also happens to be ineffectual.

Such programs appear to be directed toward curtailing questions the public has been raising about the operation and role of business in modern American society, rather than providing a forum in which these questions can be discussed.

Another response of business has been advocacy advertising, or "telling your side of the story to the public." This approach has been employed by a number of corporations, most notably Mobil Oil. While this approach has received the endorsement of the business community, it appears to have had little effect on public confidence in business. Advocacy advertising is prone to what Finlay (1979: 43) called the "Harrisburg Syndrome." In the wake of the Three Mile Island nuclear accident, the Syndrome "refers to the point where a corporation's credibility and public trust have melted down to such a low level that nobody believes anything it says anymore." Mobil's campaign is a case in point. Weiss (1978) reported on the results of a Cambridge Research poll that queried the public about their beliefs in the reliability of information from different sources about energy. The results of the survey revealed that the public rated information on energy provided by oil company spokespersons and advertising as being slightly more credible than information obtained from the lowest rated source, comic strips. While advocacy advertising may bolster morale within business, it appears to have little effect on public confidence.

The problem with these approaches to increasing public confidence is that they do not address the underlying cause of the decline. As Golden (1968: 19) observed, "The basis for public acceptance of an institution is its performance. It is not its public relations department, nor any facade it may have built . . . but the acts of the institution as a whole." Such an approach may, in fact, aggravate the problem. The data in Table 1-2 showed that mistrust in business is high. People believe that corporations are pursuing their interest (i.e., profit) at the expense of the public's interest. It is defects in performance, failures to meet the public's expectations, that have led to the decline. As Golden (1968: 4) suggested:

The lessons for corporations are clear and unmistakable. They cannot function without public consent. To obtain that consent they must act in the public interest as the public defines it at any given time. On the day that management forgets that an institution cannot exist if the general public feels that it is not useful, or that it is anti-social in the public concept of what is anti-social, the institution will begin to die.

Product recalls, unsafe toys, carcinogenic food additives, polluted air and water, bribery of domestic and foreign officials, employment discrimination, and the like have undermined public confidence. Problems such as these serve to underscore the vital point: performance is the final test of institutional legitimacy.

Effectiveness and Legitimacy

Since social legitimacy is, in a sense, the "license" for organizational existence, why do societal institutions fail to meet public demands for performance? Institutional leaders are not stupid; many rank among the best trained and most intelligent members of American society. It is not a matter of malicious intent. Institutional leaders themselves are a part of the larger public. They personally embrace and pursue the same basic sets of goals and values common to other members of society. The source of the problem lies in the way in which organizational performance is managed.

The central thesis of this book is that the decline in public confidence has been caused, in large part, by the way in which managers evaluate and control performance. Evaluation is a control mechanism within organizations and, as such, is a powerful managerial tool. The information generated by evaluations of past performance is used to direct current and future performance. The problem, simply put, is that the evaluation systems employed by organizations today do not provide managers with the kinds or quality of information necessary to guide present and future organizational action.

The primary evaluative approach employed by organizations today is the goal-based approach. In a goal-based evaluative framework, performance which attains a pre-ordained goal or goals is effective. There are a number of problems inherent in this approach. First, the goal-based approach typically represents one set of preferences for performance, usually those of organizational managers. Preferences of other relevant constituencies are not taken into consideration. While the attainment of managerial goals is important, they are not the only relevant set of preferences with respect to the impact of performance. Organizational performance is judged in many ways by the organization's constituencies regardless of whether these judgments are represented in any formal evaluative framework. Constituent judgments lie at the heart of organizational legitimacy. The constituents are the concrete linkages between an organization and the larger society. Their judgments of performance are central to the concept of legitimacy because it is from those judgments that legitimacy is derived.

If these judgments of performance are not represented in the evaluative system, constituent preferences will be ignored in directing current and future organizational performance. Ignored is perhaps too strong a term. Perceived constituent preferences will be taken into account to the degree that managers feel they are important in attaining managerial goals. This might be sufficient if performance were taking place in a static social environment and constituent preferences were predictable and stable over time. But, as was discussed earlier, society has undergone a number of fundamental changes which are reflected in qualitatively shifting constituent preferences for performance. Hence, a major problem with goal-based evaluations is that they employ a static model of organizational performance when performance takes place in a dynamic environment.

A second major shortcoming of current evaluative systems is that they do not assess performance within the context in which it occurred. It is not possible to obtain an accurate assessment of the impact of performance without an understanding of the social and environmental constraints under which an organization is operating. Social and environmental constraints act to limit what is possible in terms of performance at any given moment. Performance which may have a desirable impact at one point of time may, at another, have undesirable effects because of changes in the context in which it has occurred. The public's increased awareness of constraints on the supply of energy, for example, resulted in a downward shift in its size preferences toward more fuel efficient modes of transportation.

The problem created by assessing performance out of context is that the dynamic aspects of the impact of performance are ignored. Within a goal-based evaluative framework, context is irrelevant because the attainment of goals is the only standard against which performance is judged. The appropriateness or value of the goals is ignored. What might be effective performance today could be ineffective tomorrow because the background against which it is assessed has changed.

This book sets forth a different perspective on organizational effectiveness. It is a perspective in which the impact of organizational performance is viewed within the context of constituent preferences for performance and environmental constraints on performance. Both preferences and constraints are important in making determinations of effectiveness. Constituent preferences, in total, are a concrete representation of the public's demands for performance. Changes in constituent preferences reflect changes in the fabric of society itself, something organizations must be sensitive to if they plan to retain their social "license" to exist. Environmental constraints define what is possible in terms of organizational performance at any particular point in time. It is the evolving interaction of preferences and constraints which create the conditions organizations will face in the future.

In presenting this perspective on organizational effectiveness, the following chapter reviews existing models of effectiveness. Unlike most surveys of such models, this one focuses on the underlying element of value found in every model of effectiveness. The perspectives and value orientations of each of the major types of models are discussed and their meta criteria examined. A meta criterion can be described as the most basic value element or orientation on which a model of organizational effectiveness is based. It is the ultimate decision rule called into play to arbitrate differences among judgments of effectiveness. The meta criterion specifies the nature of the assessment of performance as well as the types of information and recommendations made from an evaluation to organizational decision makers.

Based on the critique of existing models, Chapter 3 develops a theoretical framework based on the view that judgments of effectiveness act as a selection mechanism in social evolution. Application of the Law of Requisite Variety from the field of cybernetics leads to the conclusion that the likelihood of adaptive decisions being made increases as the amount of variety in an evaluative system is increased to match the variety existing in the system being evaluated. Variety is defined as constituent preferences for organizational performance. High variety evaluations are, over time, the only way to register changes in public preferences for performance and modify organizational actions to meet changing demands.

Constituent preferences alone are insufficient for assessing organizational effectiveness. Environmental constraints bound what is possible in terms of performance as well as define the possibilities of future performance. The interaction of constraints and preferences provides the definition of what is expected, what is possible, and what is the potential of organizational performance. Only when an understanding of the preferences for and the constraints on organizational performance is gained can decision makers begin to choose among alternative actions with an eye toward adapting to and shaping the future. An evolutionary meta criterion is developed and offered as an alternative to those suggested by other models.

Two case studies are presented in Chapters 4 and 5, with the intent of clarifying, through example, the nature of the social, evolutionary, evaluative framework. The first case examines the performance of a number of small organizations in the public sector. The case describes the development, operation, and evaluation of physician extender training programs. The case begins from the perspective of a goal-based evaluator assessing performance and is expanded to incorporate the perspectives of other important program constituencies and relevant environmental constraints. The contrast between the findings of the goal-based and expanded evaluation format provides a clear illustration of the differences in conclusions reached about the effectiveness of performance using different evaluative models. The implications of the differences in results from these models for organizational decision making are examined.

The second case study presents an analysis of the automotive companies' responses to changing constituent preferences and environmental constraints during the 1970s. The analysis is based on the premise that the performance of large organizations can not be evaluated in a formal sense. Rather, large organizations have to build high variety, ongoing evaluative processes into their structure. Comparison of the relative performance of the auto companies during the 1970s provides a number of insights into the impact of high and low variety evaluative and decision processes in large organizations on organizational and social viability. The final chapter examines the differences between assessment systems designed to operate from an evolutionary perspective and contrasts them to more traditional models of evaluative research. It concludes with a discussion of the implications of the evolutionary model for strategic behavior and decision making.

2
Theory and Research on Organizational Effectiveness

Organizational effectiveness is a topic that has been of considerable importance to the administrative and organizational sciences since their inception as a field of study. Many theories of organizational processes are oriented toward creating effectively performing organizations. Interest in the concept can be traced back to early writings in the field, such as Barnard's *Functions of the Executive,* and extends to the present as witnessed by the growing numbers of articles, books, and professional meetings devoted to the topic. Much of this effort has been directed toward creating and validating a universal framework applicable to all organizations. Given the amount of attention the concept has received, it might be expected that considerable progress has been made toward this end. Unfortunately, the evidence suggests that the opposite is true. In 1966, Katz and Kahn remarked:

The literature is studded with references to efficiency, productivity, absence, turnover, and profitability—all of these offered implicitly or explicitly, separately or in combination, as definitions of organizational effectiveness. Most of what has been written on the meaning of these criteria and on their interrelatedness, however, is judgmental and open to question. What is worse, it is filled with advice that seems sagacious but is tautological and contradictory. (Katz and Kahn, 1966: 149)

Although the literature has grown considerably in the fifteen intervening years, it has not been accompanied by a corresponding growth in knowledge about the concept, nor has the state of the art much improved.

Definitions

A sampling of definitions of organizational effectiveness from frequently cited articles underscores the field's disarray. Early definitions, such as that presented by Barnard (1938: 20), defined an action as being effective "if it accomplished its specific objective aim." Generally, this is the central thrust of the goal-based approach which survives today in a more elaborate form. Price (1972: 12), for example, defined organizational effectiveness as "the degree of achievement of multiple goals," and Hannan and Freeman (1977: 110) labelled it "the degree of congruence between organizational goals and observable outcomes."

During the late 1950s, systems-based approaches were presented as an alternative to goal-based models of organizational effectiveness. These models drew on the emerging body of general systems theory which was then being introduced into the social sciences. One of the first studies employing a systems approach defined organizational effectiveness as "the extent to which an organization as a social system. . .fulfills its objectives without incapacitating its means and resources and without placing a strain upon its members" (Georgopoulos and Tannenbaum, 1957: 535). Variations on the systems theme were developed in later years and a variety of definitions within the approach appeared. Yuchtman and Seashore (1967: 898), for example, defined organizational effectiveness in terms of an organization's "bargaining position, as reflected in the ability of the organization, either in absolute or relative terms, to exploit its environment in the acquisition of scarce and valued resources."

Another stream of thought on organizational effectiveness appeared during the 1970s in the form of multiple constituency models. These models focused on constituent definitions of effectiveness. Pennings and Goodman (1977: 160), for example, suggested that organizations performed effectively if "relevant constraints [imposed by the constituencies] can be satisfied and if organizational results approximate or exceed a set of referants [criteria] for multiple goals." Other models employing this approach, such as those by Pfeffer and Salancik (1978) and Keeley (1978), proposed similar definitions.

As can be seen in the above sampling of definitions, organizational effectiveness has been defined as the attainment of goals, goal attainment without imposing strains on the organizational system, exploitation of the organization's environment for resources, and in terms of meeting criteria set by the multiple constituencies of an organization. Although there is some degree of overlap, it is apparent that a variety of thought exists on how to define organizational effectiveness.

Operationalization

Multiple definitions of organizational effectiveness would not be quite so bothersome if they simply represented different interpretations applicable to the same body of information about organizational performance. Operationalizations of the definitions reveal that disagreement on the nature of organizational effectiveness goes far beyond how it is to be defined. Campbell and his colleagues conducted a comprehensive review of the literature on organizational effectiveness published prior to 1973 and the findings of their study are instructive. First, the authors found that over twenty-five types of variables had been used as measures of effectiveness. These variables, some operationalized, others only suggested, had also been used by a number of researchers as independent variables in the process of explaining why organizations had performed effectively or ineffectively. The variables, listed in Table 2-1, indicate that organizational effectiveness has been represented in empirical work from the broadly defined category of overall effectiveness to stability, flexibility, and growth. The authors concluded:

Organizational effectiveness as it has been defined and measured in the literature is an extremely untidy construct. When twenty-five separate variables can be identified [as proxies for effectiveness] and most of these variables have several different operational forms, life becomes rather difficult. (Campbell et al., 1974: 131)

Steers' (1975) examination of seventeen multivariate models of organizational effectiveness yielded findings similar to those of Campbell et al. with respect to the heterogeneity of operational forms of the concept. The most common criteria of effectiveness were adaptability-flexibility, productivity, and satisfaction. The variables and their frequency of occurrence in the seventeen models are presented in Table 2-2. Steers noted that three quarters of these models were normative in that the authors argued that they specified the way in which organizational effectiveness *should* be assessed and that the criteria embodied in the models were meaningful and sufficient measures of the construct. Ten of the seventeen models were presented as universalistic in that they could be applied to the assessment of performance of all organizations. The remaining models were specifically designed to assess the effectiveness of business organizations. Even though each of the multivariate models employed three or four measures to represent organizational effectiveness, there was remarkably little convergence among them. In essence, both studies indicated a substantial lack of consensus as to

Table 2-1. Operational Forms of Organizational Effectiveness Identified by Campbell et al. (1974)

Overall Effectiveness
Productivity
Efficiency
Profit
Quality
Accidents
Growth
Absenteeism
Turnover
Satisfaction
Motivation
Morale
Control
Conflict/Cohesion
Flexibility/Adaptation
Goal Consensus
Role and Norm Compliance
Managerial Task Skills
Managerial Interpersonal Skills
Managerial Management and Communication
Readiness
Utilization of Environment
Evaluations by External Entities
Stability
Internalization of Organizational Goals
Value of Human Resources

SOURCE: Campbell, J. P., and E. A. Brownas, N. G. Peterson and M. D. Dunnette. *The Measurement of Organizational Effectiveness: A Review of Relevant Research and Opinion.* San Diego: Naval Personnel Research Center, 1974, pp. 39-40.

what constitutes meaningful and sufficient measures or organizational effectiveness.

Comparability Across Organizations

Questions have also been raised about the comparability of ratings of effectiveness across organizations. Hannan and Freeman (1977) argued that interorganizational comparisons of effectiveness are prone to the same problems encountered by economists in attempting to compare interpersonal utilities.[3] Goals are, in effect, preferences for performance

3. See Arrow (1951) for a classical statement of the problems inherent in comparing interpersonal utilities.

Table 2-2. Frequency of Occurrence of Evaluation Criteria in 17 Multivariate Models of Organizational Effectiveness

Evaluation Criteria	No. of Times Mentioned (N = 17)
Adaptability-Flexibility	10
Productivity	6
Satisfaction	5
Profitability	3
Resource Acquisition	3
Absence of Strain	2
Control over Environment	2
Development	2
Efficiency	2
Employee Retention	2
Growth	2
Integration	2
Open Communications	2
Survival	2
All Other Criteria	1

SOURCE: Steers, R. M., "Problems in the Measurement of Organizational Effectiveness," *Administrative Science Quarterly*, 20: (1975), p. 549.

expressed by the members of the organization. Every organization has multiple goals, some explicit, others tacit or private. Given that the preference for any goal is only weakly stated or determinable as an ordinal utility, an insurmountable problem arises in attempting to determine trade-offs between goals across raters or constituencies in judging goal attainment.[4] Hannan and Freeman argued that the severity of the problem is such that they were "in favor of dropping any pretext to scientific analysis of comparative organizational effectiveness" (1977: 131).

The type of problem that Hannan and Freeman discussed is amply demonstrated in the empirical literature. On both the inter- and intraorganizational levels of analysis, studies have found multiple, divergent goals being employed in organizational assessments. Mahoney and Weitzel (1969), for example, conducted a study on the effectiveness of general business organizations and of research and development organizations. Their findings indicated significant divergence in the criteria used to evaluate the performance of the two types of organizations.

4. Determining the trade-offs which individuals employing similar evaluative criteria make is possible (Rohrbaugh and Quinn, 1980; Hitt and Middlemist, 1979). But, it is not possible to construct trade-offs on the basis of the "utility" of criteria to raters across evaluative perspectives. This encounters the problems cited by Arrow (1951).

Managers in general business organizations employed criteria related to efficiency and productivity in judging effectiveness, while managers in research and development organizations focused on measures related to cooperative behavior, staff development, and reliable performance. Two separate models, a general business and a research and development model, were needed to explain the differences between the two sets of organizations.

Hitt and Middlemist (1979) studied managerial ratings of organizational subunit effectiveness with the specific objective of examining differences in evaluative criteria employed by managers in different subunits. Their findings were similar to those of Mahoney and Weitzel (1969) in that they indicated significant variation between managers in the criteria employed to judge subunit performance. The conclusion that can be drawn from these and similar studies is that conceptual and operational confusion abounds, in part, because there is no one universal criterion or set of criteria which can be used to assess organizational effectiveness across organizations. The results also suggest that no single criterion will be appropriate for assessing the effectiveness of a single organization.

The source of the definitional, operational, and comparability problems has been well described in the literature, although few attempts to create novel solutions have been proposed. The problem stems from the basic fact, mentioned in Chapter 1, that different individuals view organizational performance from different perspectives. Having different perspectives, individuals select different criteria against which to judge organizational performance. Mahoney and Weitzel (1969) noted that general business and research and development managers were likely to differ from each other on the basis of their values (preferences) and points of view. Explaining similar findings, Osborn and Hunt (1974: 237) observed that "in the final analysis, the overall evaluation of performance may rest on the value assumptions of the evaluator." Steers concluded his review by noting that the variety of criteria included in models of organizational effectiveness appeared to be the result of researchers trying to account for various frames of reference.

If, as these authors and others suggest, differences in perspectives or frames of reference for viewing performance lie at the heart of the problem, the search for a universal criterion or set of criteria is fruitless and ill-advised. No single set of criteria will be applicable to all organizations nor will they be viewed as applicable to all the participants judging a particular organization or action. Campbell captured the essence of this in saying that in the end organizational effectiveness is what the relevant parties decide it should be. There is no higher authority to which we can appeal. On the applied level, the task of behavioral science is to assist the people in the organization to articulate what they really mean by organizational effectiveness, show where there are gaps and inconsistencies, reveal conflicts, and help in the resolution of conflicts. This does not preclude the behavioral scientist from trying to impose his or her own value system as to what constitutes effectiveness (in modelling it), but such an assertion should be recognized for what it is. (Campbell, 1977: 52)

Models of effectiveness can be examined in terms of the perspectives or value orientations which they embody. The following provides such a review with the intent of clarifying the nature of differences among the various models offered in the literature.

Fact and Value in Judgments of Effectiveness

The terms effectiveness, evaluation, and evaluation research have been used in many different ways in the literature. This has contributed to the definitional and operational confusion. For the purpose of this discussion, an individual judgment of effectiveness is defined as a quality attributed by an individual to an activity that is perceived as having produced a desirable effect. Evaluation is a process through which this attribution is made. Suchman (1967: 11) observed, "The process of evaluating is highly complex and subjective. Inherently it involves a combination of the basic assumptions underlying the activity being evaluated and of the personal values on the part of those doing the evaluation."

Evaluative research has traditionally been defined as the application of social science methodologies to the assessment of an activity so that it is possible to determine, empirically and with the confidence that results from using scientific procedures, whether an activity has produced desired effects (Freeman, 1977; Suchman, 1967). The term is used in a much broader sense here. Evaluative research is defined as a process of inquiry in which an evaluator uses the best means and skills available to answer questions about the activity being evaluated (Williams, 1972). The difference between the two definitions of evaluative research is that the latter does not exclude other forms of inquiry, including personal inquiry. Personal inquiry need not be purely subjective. As Pondy (1977a: 5) noted: "Openness to public scrutiny and the capacity of independent verification exclude private, purely subjective forms of inquiry. But they do not exlude personal inquiry. Neither do they limit inquiry to the controlled experiment as the only fully satisfactory method of research and evaluation." Evaluation research, in other words, is being defined as a formal inquiry process in which the best methods to answer questions about the effectiveness of an activity are employed. The only caveat is that the process by which this inquiry takes place is to be public, open to scrutiny. Ideally, evaluation research objectifies the personal process of evaluation by making the assumptions underlying the activity and the personal values of those involved in the evaluation explicit and open to examination. While evaluation is subjective, evaluation research is objectifying.

The definition of effectiveness presented above is also different from those found in the literature. First, it is explicitly actor-specific and a definition of organizational effectiveness only in a very limited sense. It is a definition of organizational effectiveness only from the perspective of the individual making the judgment. The definition does not reflect an overall or systemic assessment of an activity or organization being evaluated. It describes the determination of effectiveness made by a single person, no matter who that person may be.

Second, this definition of effectiveness is based on the attribution of *desirable* effects having been produced by the activity in question rather than *desired* results. In goal-based models, effectiveness is determined by comparison of what effects were produced with what effects were desired. Use of the term desirable captures those effects that may be desired by an individual but also opens the possibility that the individual may discover other effects produced by an activity which are desirable but not originally desired. In other words, what may be desired in a situation can change as an individual receives information on what effects or outcomes an activity can or will produce. Third, the definition specifies a process through which attributions of effectiveness are made. It is a process rather than content definition of effectiveness as are those reviewed in the first chapter. Content definitions specify what an object is. Process definitions tell us how an object comes into being, and by implication, what it is.

The last distinction becomes apparent when the definition is reduced into elements of fact and value. Elements of fact consist of statements about the observable world and its operation. As Simon (1976) noted, these elements can be empirically tested to determine whether they are true or false. In the definition of effectiveness, the term "produced" connotes causality while the term "effect" connotes some state of the observable world. Both causality and the state of the world are elements of fact; they can be observed and empirically verified. For example, if an organization markets a product, a profit will result. If a school institutes a remedial reading program, students with poor reading skills will exhibit better reading skills. In both examples, causal relationships are implied and the existence of these causal relationships can be empirically examined.

Elements of value are implicit or explicit imperatives about a preferred state of a system. This is denoted in the definition of effectiveness by the term "desirable." This element of desirability cannot be completely derived from the elements of fact and cannot be proven empirically (Simon, 1976). In the above example, the desirability of earning a profit cannot be derived from the factual element that marketing a product will earn a profit. Nor can the desirability of earning a profit be empirically determined. The statement could be rearranged: "Earn a profit! You will earn a profit only when you market your product successfully." The first statement is an imperative representing a desirable state of the system, while the latter represents a causal relationship which is an element of fact. The value element provides the "colouring" of "objective reality" (Walker, 1919). In essence, value distinguishes "good" from "bad," "desirable" from "not desirable" in statements which otherwise would reflect only a cognitive mapping of reality.

Thus, the process of evaluating can be reduced into three conditions necessary for an attribution of effectiveness: (1) an effect is desirable (element of value); (2) the effect is observed or reliably predicted (element of fact); and (3) the desirable effect is perceived as having been produced by the activity being evaluated (element of fact). A judgment of effectiveness cannot be reached until all three conditions have been met. In other words, value underlies fact in evaluative judgments. An effect must be desirable, observed, or predicted, and be perceived as being produced by the activity being evaluated before it will be judged effective.

The Element of Value in Effectiveness Theory and Research

Reviews of the organizational effectiveness literature have historically proceeded by dividing it into goal-based and systems approaches (e.g., Campbell et al., 1974; Etzioni, 1960; Ghorpade, 1971; Katz and Kahn, 1966; Price, 1972; Steers, 1977). A third approach, multiple constituency or participant satisfaction models, has been added to reviews in recent years (e.g., Keeley, 1978). The position taken here is that the goal-based and systems approaches are logical extensions of each other (Webb, 1974; Campbell, 1976) while the multiple constituency models represent a departure from earlier work on organizational effectiveness. In the case of the goal-based and systems models, goal-based researchers would approach an organizational assessment by asking or discovering what the operative goals of the organization are, while the systems researcher would begin by assessing the overall strength or viability of the organization. If either group of researchers carried their assessments to their logical ends, their efforts would converge. Campbell (1977; 21-22) argued that

the goal-oriented analyst seeking to explain the organization's success or lack of success would soon have to investigate the systems variables. . . . If the natural systems analyst wonders how various systems characteristics affect task performance, he or she will have to identify tasks on which performance should be assessed. Unfortunately, in real life these second steps are often not taken. The goal-oriented analyst tends not to look in the black box, and the natural systems analyst does not like to worry about the actual task performance unless pressed.

To a degree, multiple constituency models represent an integration of the goal-based and systems approaches. Most multiple constituency models suggest tacitly that researchers need to understand organizational processes in order to determine the relevant constituent goals to be incorporated into the evaluation. Multiple constituency models are fundamentally different from the others in that they raise questions and make suggestions as to how decision makers should employ evaluative information about their organizations, given that many often conflicting sources of information are represented in the evaluative process.

Reviews of these three approaches to assessing organizational effectiveness have usually focused on the different elements of fact that models specify organizational researchers should study in making determinations of effectiveness (e.g., Campbell et al., 1974; Steers, 1975). This review treats the elements of fact specified by the models as being problematic and focuses on the elements of value embodied in the models. It is assumed that the ability of researchers to examine elements of fact in assessing effectiveness is as good as their skills and theory.

Focusing on elements of value, the literature can be classified as falling into one of three categories, labelled the "whose values," "value-free," and "multiple values" approaches. "Whose values" models are concerned with selecting the appropriate set of preferences for performance incorporation into the evaluation. Models employing a goal-based approach fall into this category. This includes the bulk of the evaluation research literature and most of the early work on organizational effectiveness. The "value-free" approach centers on the creation of "value-free" models of organizational effectiveness in that it attempts to exploit the characteristics of organizational systems as being value-free indicators of the effectiveness of organizational performance. Advocates of systems models generally fall into this category, which includes much of the literature on organizational effectiveness published in the 1960s and 1970s. A relatively small number of models fall into the "multiple values" category. These models incorporate the preferences of multiple constituencies of an organization into the assessment of effectiveness. Most of the multiple constituency models which fall into this category have been published recently and they employ a wide variety of conceptual approaches. Those which are discussed come from the organizational effectiveness literature.

"Whose Values" Approaches

The nature of goals and their selection by the evaluative researcher are central to the "whose values" approach to studying organizational effectiveness. Simon (1964) argued that goals are value premises on which organizational activities are based, and Etzioni (1964: 36) noted that they represent "a desired state of affairs that the organization attempts to realize." Given that goals represent desired outcomes or effects, the primary question of value raised in the goal-based literature has been: Whose goals are the appropriate ones to use in judging organizational effectiveness?

The debate of goal-based researchers over this question has focused on two extremes. One group has argued that evaluators should adhere to the goals set by managers of the organization in their evaluations. The other takes the position that a set of goals for the organization should be derived by evaluators based on their theory of the nature of the functional relationship between the organization and the larger social system. In the first case, Etzioni (1960) has argued that managerial goals should be used because they prevent the subjective biases of the evaluator from entering into the evaluation. Weiss and Rein (1969) and Weiss (1970) have taken the position that evaluative researchers should not become involved in the evaluation of an organization unless a clearly specified set of operational goals exists. Otherwise, they note, there is no protection from bias in the evaluation. Other researchers have cited problems inherent in attempting to use stated organizational goals (Perrow, 1961) and advocate that researchers discover the real or operative goals of the organization. These operative goals should be used in the evaluation (e.g., Freeman and Sherwood, 1970). Regardless of whether stated or operative goals are used in the evaluation, these authors are arguing that the appropriate preferences to be incorporated into evaluations or organizational effectiveness are managerial preferences.

Other authors have argued that the appropriate evaluative goals are the goals of society as derived by researchers, based on their theory of the functional relationship of the organization to society. This stream of thought is typified by the view that goal-setting is a dynamic process in which the goals reflect the relationship of the organization to the larger social system (Thompson and McEwen, 1958). As such, evaluations should reflect societal rather than managerial criteria.

Parsons' writings are most closely associated with this position. He began with the premise that the main point of departure for the analysis of organizations is its value system, which is derived from the larger society in which it is embedded (Parsons, 1956). The value pattern of the organization is conceptualized as guiding the actions of individuals within it. Its impact is felt on the organizational level through the processes by which goal-setting occurs. Hence, organizational goals should represent societal value patterns expressed in concrete functional terms and must be, in turn, legitimized by the social system. Parsons noted:

Since it has been assumed that an organization is defined by the primacy of a type of goal, the focus of its value-system must be the legitimation of this goal in terms of the functional significance of its attainment for the subordinate system, and secondly, the legitimation of the primacy of this goal over other possible interests and values of the organization and its members. (Parsons, 1956: 68)

In essence, Parsons explicitly argued that a societal perspective should be employed in making determinations of effectiveness because it is society which grants the legitimacy which allows the organization exist.

Dubin (1976) attempted to reconcile the argument over whose values should be used in evaluating organizational performance by proposing what might be termed a contingency "whose values" approach. He argued that organizational effectiveness has two meanings, depending on whether it is viewed from within or outside of the organization. As viewed from within, effectiveness could be considered the efficiency of the organization. From the outside, effectiveness may be considered more a matter of social utility. These two meanings of organizational effectiveness, Dubin noted, are not easily reconciled because the means to attain each of these ends can be very different and often contradictory. Given that the dilemma cannot be resolved, the perspective used in an evaluation becomes a matter of choice. The choice that is made is contingent upon which goal, social utility or efficiency, is preferred in a given situation. In short, different actions of an organization occur for a variety of reasons and the choice is to apply the appropriate perspective for evaluating performance contingent on the purpose of the action. Although Dubin (1976) acknowledges both the managerial and societal positions in his model, in the final analysis only one set of preferences for performance is used to evaluate organizational effectiveness.

In summary, the "whose values" debate revolves around whether a managerial or societal perspective should be used to generate criteria against which to assess organizational effectiveness. The two points of view are usually seen as irreconcilable because they focus on different facets of organizational performance which in many instances conflict. The only resolution suggested has been by Dubin (1976) in his recommendation that evaluators select the perspective most in line with the intent of the activity for the purpose of conducting the evaluation (i.e., was the action undertaken for the benefit of the organization or society?). It is obvious that elements of value form the basis for the disagreement between researchers as to what "facts," as derived from the comparison of performance against evaluative criteria, should be considered in arriving at judgments of organizational effectiveness.

"Value-Free" Approaches

"Value-free" models of organizational effectiveness usually embody a general systems approach to the study of organizations. These models arose, in large part, out of a desire to avoid the value selection problems inherent in "whose values" models discussed above. A major shift in emphasis in the elements of fact examined in models of effectiveness occurred with the creation of "value-free" models. "Value-free" models focused on information related to organizational processes while "whose values" approaches examined information on the attainment of desired ends.

The first major article employing a "value-free" model was published in 1957 by Georgopoulos and Tannenbaum in a study of the effectiveness of an industrial service organization. They created a model of organizational effectiveness based on organizational functions, as opposed to organizational goals, with two explicit purposes: (1) to avoid the "whose values" dilemma and (2) to construct a model applicable to all organizations. Since then, the use of the systems approach as a basis for "value-free" models has increased, as evidenced by the growing number of systems or functional models of effectiveness (e.g., Etzioni, 1960; Evan, 1976; Katz and Kahn, 1966; Steers, 1977; Yuchtman and Seashore, 1967). The models developed by Katz and Kahn (1966), Yuchtman and Seashore (1967), and Evan (1976) are illustrative of the logic underlying the "value-free" approach and its treatment of the element of value.

Katz and Kahn's (1966) version of the systems model is widely cited in the literature and representative of the use of the systems approach in the study of organizational effectiveness. The systems approach is concerned with the problems of relationships, or structures and their interdependence within a system. Systems, such as organizations, are characterized as: (1) being nested within larger systems; (2) importing, transforming, and exporting energy (inputs, transformations, and outputs) with their environments to avoid decay (negative entropy); (3) able to reach a given state (homeostasis) by a number of paths (equifinality); (4) having complex feedback and regulatory mechanisms that permit adaptive responses to changes in their environments; and (5) social activities are viewed as patterned cycles of events rather than the behaviors of individual actors. Katz and Kahn (1966) argued that, within this framework, organizational effectiveness reflects the degree to which an organization maximizes all forms of energetic return (i.e., inputs and outputs) in its relationship with the environment. A distinction is often made between efficiency and external activities that promote maximization of energetic return. Katz and Kahn (1966), for example, noted that organizations need to be both "politically effective" and internally "efficient." In a more general sense, effectiveness within the systems approaches can be conceptualized as the ability of an organization to meet its goals rather than actual goal attainment. This emphasis is directed toward the system's ability to survive, or toward means rather than ends. Etzioni (1960) suggested that systems models of effectiveness are concerned with selecting the comparatively best path for organizational survival.

Yuchtman and Seashore (1967) presented a variation on the general systems theme in their resource acquisition model of organizational effectiveness. They view organizations in a manner similar to Katz and Kahn (1966) by focusing on organizational processes rather than organizational ends. Effectiveness was defined as the bargaining position of a firm with respect to its environment, and its ability to exploit its environment in the acquisition of scarce and valued resources. Goals are viewed as strategies adopted by the organizational members to enhance the organization's bargaining position with the environment rather than as desired outcomes. The focus on resource attainment considers only one of the three major processes of the organization/environment relationship (i.e., inputs and not transformations or outputs); but, Yuchtman and Seashore (1967) argued that the focus on the organization's bargaining position is relevant to all three processes, and, as such, reflects them. They also suggest that the only area in which the effectiveness of dissimilar organizations can be compared is on their success in procuring scarce and valued resources. Hence, the highest level of effectiveness is reached when the organization maximizes its bargaining position and maximizes resource procurement.

A third "value-free" model was presented by Evan (1976) in what could be termed a systems efficiency model of organizational effectiveness. The organization was characterized as a "goal-setting, goal-seeking, goal-changing type of social system . . . [that] is in the process of changing its initial condition from one time period to the next. . . ." (Evan, 1976: 20). Evan assumed that all organizational social systems had at least four major cyclical processes in common: (1) inputs of the various types of resources; (2) transformations of resources with the aid of social and or technical processes; (3) outputs which are transmitted to other social systems; and (4) feedback effects from the environment. Nine ratios, representing different relationships between inputs, outputs, and transformations, were presented as candidates for effectiveness measures in that they reflected the state of the organization longitudinally and cross-sectionally. These ratios were viewed as providing information necessary for decision makers to adjust organizational processes in order to minimize or maximize the values associated with "universal" input, transformation, and output goals. Hence, within this model, Evan characterized organizational effectiveness as the capacity of the organization to cope with all four systemic processes relative to its goal-seeking behavior.

It is clear from the above that systems models shifted the factual focus of evaluation research from organizational ends to organizational processes. It was assumed that, since these processes were common to all organizations, the models provided a value-free method of assessing organizational effectiveness. In reality, this was more a matter of the element of value being submerged than being eliminated. Elements of value became the core assumptions of systems models of effectiveness. Core assumptions are the foundation upon which any approach or theory is built. They subsume a certain state of the world or reality. While these assumptions themselves are not questions, open to empirical examination, or rarely discussed, the hypotheses derived from them are amenable to empirical investigation (Lakatos, 1970). Hence, most researchers employing systems models of organizational effectiveness (e.g., Evan, 1976; Mahoney and Frost, 1974; Mott, 1972; Duncan, 1973; Neghandi and Reimann, 1973) assumed that their models were value-free.[5]

The error in this particular line of reasoning was that organizational effectiveness is, by nature, a value-based concept. All judgments of effectiveness, as noted earlier, contain an element of value. Treating it as a value-free concept creates a problem in that a fundamental issue concerning effectiveness (i.e., elements of value) is ignored and an assumption is made that "objective" measures of organizational effectiveness can be created without reference to values. The danger in this, as Campbell (1977: 45-56) noted, is that

the conventional wisdom says that objectivity is good, but a perhaps more accurate wisdom says an objective criterion is a subjective criterion one step removed. . . . Subjective judgments can be found in *any* so-called objective measure of effectiveness, which makes using 'available' objective measures (where the subjectivity is unknown) as criteria in a research study very risky business.

By the early 1970s the situation concerning the state of the art on organizational effectiveness became increasingly confused. Goal-based models of effectiveness raised questions as to whether managerial or societal perspectives should be employed in evaluating organizational performance. With the introduction of systems models, the perspective of organizational scientists entered the discussion. Spray (1976) captured the state of the field well in her description of the 1975 Kent State Conference on organizational effectiveness. She noted that major prob-

5. Another version of the systems approach that avoids the problem of values encountered in Katz and Kahn's (1966) model has been presented by Churchman (1968). In Churchman's model, the researcher is simply another part of the system and the question of "whose" goals are appropriate for the evaluation is explicit and important. Churchman's model of the systems approach is not generally recognized within organizational theory. For example, a review of the references for twelve articles on organizational effectiveness in *Administrative Science Quarterly* (March, 1970, through December, 1980) showed that two-thirds reference Katz and Kahn (1966) while none cite Churchman (1968).

lems in communication arose between the organizational scientists and managers attending the conference. The problems revolved around the qualitatively different criteria used by each group to discuss the concept of organizational effectiveness. The managers were concerned with the attainment of organizational ends while the scientists were concerned with organizational processes. Even though there was variation in the opinions and beliefs within each group, it was much less than there was between them. Spray observed that the fairly common set of evaluative criteria held by the organizational scientists simply rejected the fact that "they have had highly similar educational experiences which qualify them for membership in a 'community of scholars' who are highly likely to develop similar constructions of organizational reality" (1976: 19).

In short, organizational scientists have their own particular perspective on organizational performance. Their perspective is simply one of many that can enter into evaluations of organizational effectiveness. In their attempt to create value-free models of organizational effectiveness, organizational scientists simply injected their own values rather than eliminating values altogether.

"Multiple Values" Approaches

There was a growing sense of dissatisfaction with the state of theory and research on organizational effectiveness within the organizational sciences during the 1970s, as evidenced by the critical reviews which appeared in the literature (e.g., Dubin, 1976; Steers, 1975; Campbell et al., 1974; Campbell, 1976, 1977). As a result, multiple constituency models of effectiveness began to appear in the literature. In their general form, multiple constituency models view organizations as "intersections of particular influence loops, each embracing a constituency biased toward assessment of the organization's activities in terms of its own exchanges within the loop" (Connolly et al., 1980: 215). Hence, the criteria used in judging organizational performance in these models reflect the nature of constituent interactions with the organization.

The first major examination of this perspective grew out of the Carnegie-Mellon workshop on organizational effectiveness held in 1976. The proceedings of the workshop contained the first formal model employing a multiple constituency perspective (Pennings and Goodman, 1977). Since that time, a number of models and discussions of the multiple constituency perspective have appeared (e.g., Pfeffer and Salancik, 1978; Hrebiniak, 1978; Keeley, 1978; Connolly et al., 1980). Although these models are relatively new in terms of viewing organizational effectiveness from multiple points of view, their substantive orientation can be traced back to two early articles, by Bass (1952) and Friedlander and Pickle (1967).

Bass (1952) was one of the earliest proponents of expanding the conceptualization of organizational effectiveness. He suggested that the criterion of "organizational success" needed to be expanded to include measures relevant to employees, society as a whole, and to the organization's management. Criteria which were suggested for inclusion into assessments of organizational performance were to reflect: 1) the degree to which an organization was profitable, productive, etc.; 2) the degree to which the organization was of value to its employees; and 3) the degree to which the organization and its members were of value to society.

Bass believed that these three sets of criteria were unlikely to be highly correlated and that the value of the organization to its employees and the value of an organization to society should be considered on their own merit. Stated in axiomatic form, Bass noted that his proposition could be neither empirically proved nor disproved. Rather, he argued that the proposition was widely accepted in a number of areas overlapping industrial psychology, namely, law, industrial and labor relations, and the military services. The tenor of the argument was that in each of these areas the needs of both the members of the organization and society are considered in decision making. Bass concluded:

Although the point of view expressed is in itself a value judgment, subject to arbitrary acceptance or rejection, it is consonant with the legal and philosophical attitude which has enabled capitalism to survive as a productive, progressive economic system in this country. It is also consonant with the humanistic and moral attitudes toward the individual which prevail here. Thus, acceptance of the proposed axiom will enable the industrial psychologist to formally adopt some of the values about the individual the majority of the nation holds—which the industrial psychologist as a private citizen does consider, but which he has not incorporated into his evaluation of his own professional services. (Bass, 1952)

Friedlander and Pickle (1967) empirically examined Bass' belief that the criteria important to different constituencies were unlikely to be highly correlated in a study of ninety-seven small businesses. They based their conceptualization on the premise that organizations are highly interdependent with their environment and that criteria for assessing effectiveness should reflect those interdependencies and their management. These interdependencies were viewed as exchange relationships, and as such, both the organization's contribution to society and its ability to maximize its return from society needed to be incorporated into assessments of effectiveness. Following Bass' line of argument, they suggested:

Clearly effectiveness criteria must take into account the profitability of the organization, the degree to which it satisfies its members, and the degree to which it is of value to the larger society of which it is a part. These three perspectives include systems maintenance and growth, subsystem fulfillment, and environmental fulfillment. Each is obviously composed of several related components, and each component is hypothetically related to the other. (Friedlander and Pickle, 1967: 293)

Several constituent perspectives, those of the firm's owner, employees, customers, creditors, suppliers, the community, and government, were incorporated into the study. Criteria were generated and scales developed to reflect each constituent's perspective. The matrix of intercorrelations between the criteria generated from the constituent perspectives revealed that the fulfillment of one constituency's preferences for performance was not likely to be highly related to the fulfillment of other constituencies' preferences. Seven of twenty-one correlations were significantly positive, the highest being ($r = .37$) between the satisfaction of owner and customer preferences. Three other correlations were negative, although not significantly so. The authors concluded that organizations probably find it difficult to simultaneously fulfill the variety of demands made upon them and that it is unlikely that they attempt to maximize the fulfillment of any one constituency's preferences for performance. Rather, Friedlander and Pickle (1967) argued that organizations probably operate using policies which attempt to minimally fulfill the preferences of several constituencies simultaneously.

Neither Bass nor Friedlander and Pickle attempted to address the question of what organizational effectiveness was from the multiple constituency perspective. They focused on the variety of constituent perspectives necessary for judging organizational effectiveness and the degree to which these perspectives were interrelated. Models which began to apper in the 1970s built on this earlier work by accepting the underlying premises embodied in it. The later models attempted to develop an understanding of the nature of organizational effectiveness within the multiple constituency framework and explore the concept's implications for organizational decision making. Even though they are similar in underlying structure, the models have a number of fundamental differences in terms of how they employ the approach and their considerations of the nature of organizational effectiveness.

Disagreement among multiple constituency models is based on the meta criteria the models employ. A meta criterion is the ultimate decision rule employed by these models in determining how the effectiveness of organizational performance is to be judged and what the implications of the evaluative information are for managerial action. The reason that the issue of meta criteria surfaces with these models and not with the earlier goal-based or systems models is that the latter employ only a single value-based perspective of organizational performance while the multiple constituency models embrace multiple value perspectives of performance. In the single perspective models, the meta criterion is implicit in the value perspective chosen for evaluation, regardless of whether it is the perspective of managers, society, or organizational scientists. The decision rule for judging organizational effectiveness is one of meeting the preferences of the given constituency. The implication for organizational decision making and action is that performance should be modified to satisfy the preferences of the given constituency.

Consider the logic inherent in a managerially oriented, goal-based model of organizational effectiveness. The value perspective embodied in the model is that of managers. The criteria employed in the assessment of performance are chosen to reflect managerial goals (preferences) for performance. The organization, according to the logic of the model, has performed effectively if these goals are attained. If the goals have not been attained, the implication for action is straightforward. You modify the performance of the organization to fulfill the managerial preferences. In short, the decision rule for making both the determination of organizational effectiveness and the implications for the use of the evaluative information in guiding organizational action are implicit in the logic of the model itself.

This simplicity is not the case in multiple constituency models of organizational effectiveness, because they embrace multiple value-perspectives on the desirability of organizational performance. As Friedlander and Pickle's study showed, multiple perspectives on performance are more likely to be divergent than convergent. By incorporating multiple views of performance, the questions of what is effective organizational performance and what are implications of the judgment and evaluative information for organizational action are no longer straightforward. In effect, the evaluator and/or the organizational decision maker has to make an explicit choice. Generally, this choice is perceived as one of selecting one set of constituent preferences as representing "organizational effectiveness." The multiple constituency models, therefore, explicitly raise the issue of meta criteria because a choice has to be made.

Three meta criteria, based on the notions of relativism, power, and social justice, are clearly identifiable in the multiple constituency literature. Briefly, the relativistic meta criterion takes the position that no judgment of organizational effectiveness can be made, nor can the evaluator provide the decision maker with any advice on how the information should be interpreted to guide organizational action. The power meta criterion specifies that effective organizational performance satisfies the preferences of the most powerful constituencies of the organization. The social justice meta criterion, on the other hand, implies that effective organizational performance is that which fulfills the preferences of the least advantaged constituency of the organization. The identification of these meta criteria in multiple constituency models is sometimes explicit in the description of the nature of organizational effectiveness, but more often apparent in their discussions of how decision makers should use the evaluative information in guiding organizational performance. The discussion of multiple constituency models below focuses on these differences in meta criteria.

Relativism as a Meta Criterion

Relativism is a special case in the classification system of meta criteria. Relativistic multiple constituency models view the approach as an empirical technique used in the collection of information on organizational performance. The model presented by Connolly et al. (1980) can be most closely associated with this position. As an empirical technique, the multiple constituency approach is viewed as a method by which to collect data about constituent preferences for and their judgments about organizational performance. An overall judgment of organizational effectiveness is viewed as being neither possible nor desirable given the multitude of constituent perspectives. Although not explicit in the model, it can be assumed that some type of evaluative report would be passed on to organizational decision makers, without comment, to use as they please.

The important point of the relativistic position in relation to this discussion is that it highlights the nature of the meta criteria employed by other models. In splitting apart the empirical and the normative elements of multiple constituency models, Connolly and his colleagues correctly noted that meta criteria are concerned with distributive issues concerning organizational outcomes. The distributive issue in this case is the distribution of "satisfactions" of constituent preferences for organizational performance. Although they indicated that they were uncomfortable with the use of any normative criterion to reduce multiple evaluations into a summary statement on organizational effectiveness, Connolly et al. (1980) noted distributional issues open up a range of empirical questions about organizations, constituencies, and their interactions.

Power as a Meta Criterion

The meta criterion of power is mostly closely associated with the models and discussions of organizational effectiveness presented by Pennings and Goodman (1977), Pfeffer and Salancik (1978), and Hrebiniak (1978). The use of power as a meta criterion is most clearly expressed in the model formulated by Pennings and Goodman (1977). Their conceptualization was based upon Thompson's (1967) concept of a dominant coalition composed of various internal interest groups. These interest groups are seen as defining effectiveness by constructing referents (criteria) against which an organization's performance is measured. The degree to which any interest group can impose its set of referents on the organization is a function of its position in the organization's power structure. The power of each interest group is determined by: (1) its ability to cope with uncertainty facing the organization; (2) the degree to which other interest groups are substitutable for it; and (3) the degree to which the interest group is central or critical to the functioning of the organization. Accordingly, the more powerful the interest group, the more likely that it will have its preferences for performance satisfied over those of other members of the dominant coalition. Interest groups are also seen as acting as determinants of an organization's effectiveness through their ability to affect the organization's well-being, which implies control over some critical input, transformation process, or output. External interest groups can impose constraints on an organization which limit its behavior (e.g., government regulation, competitors' actions).

In essence, the dominant coalition acts as an arena in which various interest groups bargain or negotiate the referents, goals, and constraints to be accepted by them as the substantive definition of an organization's effectiveness. The dominant coalition synthesizes the preferences of the various interest groups into a single, aggregate perspective of organizational performance. Thus, effective organizational performance is defined as performance satisfying the negotiated preferences of the dominant coalition within which the preferences of the organization's most powerful constituencies are weighted most heavily.

Pfeffer and Salancik (1978) approach the question of organizational effectiveness from a somewhat different tack in that they do not explicitly address the question of what overall organizational effectiveness is. Rather, they noted that each organizational constituency defines effectiveness according to its own perspective of performance. They also make an important distinction between effectiveness and efficiency. Effectiveness is defined as the degree to which the organization is fulfilling the needs or satisfying the criteria of various evaluators *external* to the organization, while efficiency is seen as an *internal* standard of organizational performance. The major difference beween their model and that of Pennings and Goodman is that Pennings and Goodman argue that organizational effectiveness is defined by the constituencies internal to the organization, while Pfeffer and Salancik view it as an externally imposed standard.

The power meta criterion is evident in Pfeffer and Salancik's model in both the underlying rationale for the model and the advice given to decision makers for the use of evaluative information. The model of effectiveness is predicated on what Pfeffer and Salancik see as the central questions concerning organizational action: "Who wants what and how important is it that the demand be satisfied? And what are the implications of the satisfaction of one demand for the satisfaction of other demands?" (Pfeffer and Salancik, 1978: 87). In terms of advice for the organizational decision makers, Pfeffer and Salancik specify a four step process for the collection and utilization of evaluative information.

The first step is the identification of organizational constituencies. Pfeffer and Salancik note that constituencies may be of unequal importance to an organization; so as a second step, it is necessary for the manager to develop a system for weighting the relative importance of each to the organization. The suggested method for assigning weights to the constituencies is drawn from the resource dependence framework developed by these authors earlier (Salancik and Pfeffer, 1974; Pfeffer and Salancik, 1974). The general thrust of the resource dependence model is that constituencies controlling resources critical to the functioning of an organization have power over the organization because it is dependent on the constituency for the resource. As a result, more attention should be paid to the demands of powerful constituencies. After weighting the relative importance of the constituencies to the organization, the third step would be to identify the criteria or preferences for performance that each of these constituent groups would employ in judging performance. Once the criteria or preferences for performance have been identified, the manager would move to the final step of the evaluative process and determine what the reaction of each constituency would be to any particular organizational action. The implied end point is that the decision maker should attend to the preferences of the most powerful organizational constituencies because they control resources critical to its continued operation. Hence, performance which satisfies the demands or preferences of an organization's most powerful constituencies is effective.

Hrebiniak's (1978) discussion of organizational effectiveness proceeds much along the same lines as that of Pfeffer and Salancik. The major difference is that Hrebiniak explicitly addresses the question concerning the nature of an overall judgment of organizational effectiveness. He argued that

it may be useful to think in terms of *effectivenesses*. The organization typically is evaluated on a number of fronts, and the criteria of performance and decisions regarding outcome may vary a great deal. Again, the process is political. The organization uses or recognizes power as it tries to show historical improvement, show a good relative standing, or stress especially visible, popular, or important criteria to its various publics.(Hrebiniak, 1978: 326)

In short, models employing the power meta criterion take the position, implicitly or explicitly, that effective organizational performance is that which satisfies the preferences of the most powerful organizational constituencies. In satisfying these preferences, the organization is assuring itself of a continued supply of critical resources and the participation of those constituencies on which it is dependent.

Social Justice as a Meta Criterion

Keeley (1978) presented a model of organizational effectiveness employing a social justice meta criterion which was derived from Rawls' (1971) theory of justice. Rawls viewed a just society as being one in which "all social values—liberty and opportunity, income and wealth, and the bases of self-respect—are distributed equally unless an unequal distribution of any, or all, of these values is to everyone's advantage" (1971: 62). Rawls derived two principles from this conceptualization of social justice against which alternative social arrangements could be judged. The first principle stated that each person within a society has an equal right to the most extensive system of basic liberties compatible with a similar system of liberty for all. The second principle stated that social and economic inequities within a society should be arranged so that they are both: 1) to the benefit of the least advantaged members of that society subject to the first principle; and 2) attached to offices and positions which are open to all members of society under conditions of fair equality of opportunity.

As House (1980) noted, this conceptualization of justice limits the ends which a society can seek and the means by which the ends can be attained. Such a formulation of justice would preclude imposing disadvantages on the few for the benefit of the many. Given that the first principle (i.e., every individual has a right to an extensive system of rights of which they can not be deprived) has priority over the second, basic liberties are to be maximized without regard to social and economic benefits. Provided that the first principle is met, then social and economic inequalities may be allowed, but only if they benefit the least advantaged within the society. In any event, Rawls' concept of justice does not allow inequalities if they do not benefit the least advantaged nor can trade-offs be made between basic liberties and social or economic advantages. Applied to evaluation, House (1980) noted that this specifies that the perspective of a "representative least advantaged person" would be singled out to provide the standard against which to judge performance. Keeley (1978) operationalized the concept of social justice through a minimum regret principle. In essence, the effective organization would seek to minimize constituents' regret over the actual consequences of their participation in the organization. Comparatively, the most effective organization would be that which has the least most regretful constituency.

The problem with this operationalization is that it violates Rawls' notion of justice in a number of situations. Connolly et al. (1980), for example, noted that under this operationalization, a prison in which the prisoners (the least advantaged constituency) were dissatisfied would have to be judged as ineffective. The minimum regret principle also encounters problems when it is used to compare the effectiveness of organizations. Consider a hypothetical evaluation of two organizations which train the hard-core unemployed. For the purpose of discussion assume that there are two relevant constituencies included in the evaluation process, the trainees and the labor unions whose domain is the trade in which the trainees are being trained. The evaluator would select a sample of persons representing the views of these constituencies and determine the extent to which each constituency regretted its participation in the organization. The results might reveal that 20 percent of the trainees in both organizations regretted their participation. Fifty percent of the labor union constituency regretted their participation with Organization A while only 20 percent regretted their participation with Organization B.

Suppose our hypothetical evaluator probed a little further in order to determine why such a disparity existed between the labor union constituencies and found that the union constituency of Organization A regretted their participation because it was training people to compete with them in the labor market. In spite of pressure from the union, the training organization continued to train people in this skill area. A similar situation was found to exist between the union and Organization B, but the union had been successful in getting the organization to shift the focus of its training to another skill area. While the trainees of this program did not compete directly with the members of the union, they were being trained in skills for which fewer jobs were available. As a result, some of the trainees were unable to find employment after completion of the training program.

If Keeley's guidelines of the minimum regret principle are applied to this scenario, Organization B would be judged as performing more effectively than Organization A because it has minimized the regret of the participating constituencies. If Rawls' principles were applied, Organization A would be the more effective because it would be arranging economic inequities to the benefit of the least advantaged constituency of the organization, the trainees. While the notion of minimizing regret has some appeal as an operational representation of social justice, it encounters problems in that it can lead to violations of Rawls' principles. Operational problems aside, the social justice criterion is one which specifies that effective organizational performance is that which benefits the least advantaged constituency of that organization.

Meta Criteria and Social Legitimacy

These meta criteria present distinctly different ways of viewing and evaluating organizational performance. It is obvious that there is significant disgreement as to what effective performance is and what the implications of these judgments are for managerial action. A better understanding of differences and problems inherent in these models can be attained by examining them in the context of the nature of judgments of organizational effectiveness. The relationship beween judgments of effectiveness and social legitimacy hinges on the notion that judgments of effectiveness concern the distribution of "organizational goods" in terms of the degree to which an organization satisfies constituent preferences for performance. To paraphrase Pfeffer and Salancik, the central issue is one of who gets what and what the implications are of the satisfaction of some constituents' preferences over others. Decisions about the distribution of "organizational goods" present organizational decision makers with what Rittel and Weber (1973) call "wicked problems." The following analysis draws heavily on Rittel and Weber's distinction between wicked and tame problems and their discussion of the nature of wicked problems.

Rittel and Weber (1973) describe two types of problems which professionals such as planners, evaluators, and managers encounter in their professions. Tame problems are those that usually concern scientists and engineers: they are clearly definable and a solution can be generated.

As an example, consider a problem of mathematics, such as solving an equation; or the task of an organic chemist in analyzing the structure of some unknown compound; or that of the chessplayer attempting to accomplish checkmate in five moves. For each the mission is clear. It is clear, in turn, whether or not the problems have been solved. (Rittel and Weber, 1973: 160)

Generally, tame problems are those for which a "correct" formulation of the problem is possible, and in turn, for which a correct solution is attainable.

Wicked problems present a different tableau for the decision makers. They are problems which are not characterized as being clearly definable or having a correct solution, such as decisions concerning the distribution of "organizational goods" in the satisfaction of constituent preferences for performance. There are many ways to formulate a wicked problem and many possible answers. These problems have no clear solution and, as Rittel and Weber noted, wicked problems are never "solved." They can, at best, be "re-solved" over and over again. A solution selected at one time does not solve a wicked problem; it simply keeps it from resurfacing for a while. Rittel and Weber (1973) presented a number of propositions about the nature of wicked problems which clarify their nature. The following discussion of nature of wicked problems reveals the shortcomings of current models of organizational effectiveness.

1. *There is no definitive formulation for a wicked problem.* There are many possible formulations or characterizations of wicked problems, as opposed to one "correct" formulation of a tame problem. Rittel and Weber (1973: 160) noted: "The choice of an explanation [of a wicked problem] is arbitrary in a logical sense. People choose explanations which are most plausible to them." As noted earlier, constituent definitions of organizational effectiveness are based on their preferences for performance, which is the most plausible aspect of performance for them to judge since it directly affects them. Evaluators define the problem of what organizational effectiveness is in accordance with their perceptions of and preferences for organizational performance, regardless of whether they be constituents of the organization or professional evaluators.

Problem definition is important because, as Rittel and Weber point out, the formulation of the problem defines its solution. "The formulation of the wicked problem is the problem! The process of formulating the problem and of conceiving a solution (or re-solution) are identical, since every specification of the problem is a specification of the direction in which a treatment (action) is considered" (Rittel and Weber, 1973: 161). This becomes obvious when the meta criteria embodied in different models of organizational effectiveness are compared. The meta criterion itself specifies what actions or treatments the organizational decision maker should consider in modifying performance. The social justice meta criterion, for example, specifies that actions be taken to benefit the least advantaged, while the power meta criterion indicates that the interests of the most powerful should be served. With the exception of the relativistic model, the meta criteria define the problem by applying a particular perspective. The solution to the "problem" then becomes obvious. Selecting a meta criterion for an evaluation of performance is perhaps the most important step of the evaluative process. Once it is selected, problem definition becomes relatively simple as does creating possible solutions to the evaluative problem.

The meta criterion also specifies the types of facts about the organization that an evaluator will examine in describing the system and reaching a specific solution. The use of different meta criteria in evaluating performance will result in different descriptions of performance. The power meta criterion will probably result in more information about the preferences of powerful constituencies and less about the preferences of the least advantaged in the evaluations. The opposite would be true in evaluations employing a social justice meta criterion. It is difficult to predict a description of organizational performance when a relativistic perspective prevails, since ostensibly it prescribes no point of view. It is likely that the criteria selected, or perhaps the constituencies selected to be included in the evaluation, will vary according to each individual evaluator's point of view. The inherent danger is that this camouflages the element of value incorporated into the evaluation while the other meta criteria implicitly or explicitly define the value orientation being employed.

2. *Wicked problems have no stopping rules.* Since there are definitive solutions to tame problems, a decision maker knows when a solution has been reached because of the presence of solution-testing criteria. This is not the case with wicked problems. No definitive solution to a wicked problem can be reached because a definitive formulation of the problem itself cannot be made. Given that selecting the problem formulation is the same as selecting a solution and no definitive formulation can be generated, work on solving the problem is stopped because of reasons external to the logic of the problem-solving process itself. For example, the stopping point for evaluations is usually defined by such things as a lack of additional time, lack of funds, or a judgment that the solution generated by the evaluation process is "good enough." A solution to an evaluative problem can be found but it is not *the* solution. It is simply one of many possible solutions.

3. *Solutions to wicked problems are not true-or-false, but good or bad.* The solutions to tame problems can be checked to see whether they provide a correct answer. The solution or solution set for a mathematical equation can be checked to determine whether or not it has actually solved the problem. Chess strategies can be tested to determine whether they will result in checkmate. Correct answers are possible for tame problems because criteria can be generated against which the solution can be tested.

Again, this is not the case with wicked problems such as those dealing with the satisfaction of different constituents' preferences. As Rittel and Weber (1973: 163) noted:

Normally, many parties are equally equipped, interested, and or entitled to judge the solution [to a wicked problem] although none has the power to set formal decision rules to determine correctness. Their judgments are likely to differ widely to accord with their group or personal interests, their special value-sets, and their ideological predilections. Their assessment of proposed solutions are expressed as "good" or "bad" or, more likely, as "better or worse" or "satisfying" or "good enough."

Constituents of an organization will judge the "goodness" of judgments of organizational effectiveness and organizational actions based on their performance preferences. Correct solutions are impossible since there are no criteria for selecting among the competing perspectives. Judgments and actions stemming from them all will be assessed by each constituency as being better or worse, good or bad, satisfying or not satisfying, good or not good enough. They cannot be judged as being correct-incorrect, since there is no basis for that judgment.

To elevate one constituent perspective above the others in the evaluative process says, in effect, that one constituent group's view of performance is the correct or true one. This creates what Bateson (1972) refers to as an error in logical typing. Simply put, a classification cannot be the same as one of its members. The term tree, for example, is a general classification with many members such as oak, elm, spruce, and poplar. It is incorrect to refer to all trees as oaks since there are many other members in the classification. There is a difference between members of a classification and the classification per se. Similarly, it is incorrect to define the overall classification of "organizational effectiveness" as one of the members of the classification, i.e., constituent judgments of effectiveness. The managerial, systems, power, and social justice meta criteria all fall into this error of classification. Each says that organizational effectiveness is the same as the perspective on which the judgment of effectiveness is based. The perspective of one constituency is being raised, in each instance, to the level of the overall classification. If organizational effectiveness is to be a useful concept, it must be something more than one of the constituent judgments.

4. *There is no immediate and no ultimate test to the solution of a wicked problem.* Solutions to wicked problems "generate waves of consequences over an extended—virtually an unbounded—period of time" (Rittel and Weber, 1973: 163). These effects may be either positive or negative in terms of the types of impacts that were desired or expected. Since the full consequences of an action taken to solve a wicked problem are unlikely ever to be fully known, a determination of the ultimate effect of a solution is impossible.

With regard to evaluators and organizational decision makers employing such information, the effects of actions taken based on evaluative information can never be fully appraised. The solution to one wicked problem may, in turn, create other wicked problems. The dimension of time also affects evaluations. Today's evaluation will generate actions to remedy perceived deficiencies in performance. By tomorrow, those actions may have created other deficiencies as judged by the organization's constituencies, which requires solving still "another" wicked problem. Hence, wicked problems are never solved. Rather, they are in constant need of re-solving. In effect, the actions managers take today create the problems they face in the future.

5. *Every attempted solution counts significantly.* In the case of tame problems, problem solvers test various solutions to see if they work. If a solution does not work (i.e., it is incorrect) another is generated and tried. The costs of experimenting with different solutions to a mathematical equation are quite low.

Every solution to a wicked problem leaves "traces" in the system which cannot be undone once it has been implemented. If the solution has not had the desired effect the decision maker has to face a new version of the system, one which was in part created by the earlier action. As Rittel and Weber (1973: 163) noted: "Whenever actions are effectively irreversible and whenever the half-lives of the consequences are long, *every trial counts*. And every attempt to reverse a decision or to correct for undesired consequences poses another set of wicked problems which in turn are subject to the same dilemmas."

6. *Every wicked problem is essentially unique.* Tame problems can often be classified on the basis of similarities in their properties. Given the similarities, general solutions or solution sets can often be formulated which are effective in solving all the problems falling into that particular class. Mathematical problems, for example, can be classified according to certain well defined sets of characteristics which are common to mathematical problems, and a solution or solution set can be devised which solves all the problems within the classification.

Wicked problems may exhibit many similarities but there is typically one characteristic of a problem which will make it unique. The unique characteristic can be critical in determining the efficacy of a solution. Often, critical differences between wicked problems are contextual. Rittel and Weber cited an example of applying the design of a mass transit system designed for one area to another. While the underlying problem of providing mass transit is similar for different areas, the context of the community in which the design is to be applied is an overriding factor which outweighs the similarities. Using the mass transit system design for the city of Chicago in Detroit, for example, is likely to be inappropriate given the unique characteristics of the two metropolitan areas.

Similarly, evaluative problems are unique because the context in which organizational performance and its evaluation take place varies from organization to organization. What might be appropriate for one organization in terms of a judgment of effectiveness and corresponding recommendations for action may be entirely inappropriate for another because of contextual differences. And what is appropriate at one point of time for a single organization can also change as the context in which performance takes place changes. None of the evaluative models discussed earlier take the factor of context into account in their portrayals of the evaluative process.

7. *The evaluator has no right to be wrong.* This paraphrased version of Rittel and Weber's last proposition presents one of the most provocative statements in their discussion of wicked problems. They noted that the task of professionals such as planners, evaluators, and so on is fundamentally different from that of the basic scientist. Within the realm of science, solutions to problems are viewed as hypotheses offered for refutation. The larger the number of studies which do not contain refutations of a particular hypothesis, the more confidence the scientific community places in its validity or correctness.

The goal of professionals such as evaluators and planners "is not to find truth, but to improve some characteristics of the world where people live. Planners [and evaluators] are liable for the consequences of the actions they generate; the effects can matter a great deal to the people that are touched by those actions" (Rittel and Weber, 1973: 167). In essence, evaluators do have an ethical responsibility. Even though there are no right answers for wicked problems they evaluate, the actions generated on the basis of their evaluations affect the lives of other people. They have a responsibility to assist decision makers in finding solutions to wicked problems which better satisfy constituent preferences as they evolve over time.

Within the context of "organizational effectiveness as a wicked problem," the shortcomings of existing models become clear. Evaluations of performance are used by organizational decision makers in resolving problems of "who gets what" from an organization in terms of the satisfaction of constituent preferences. Organizational legitimacy is dependent on the satisfaction of these preferences. If an organization does not satisfy constituent preferences for performance it will lose the basis for its legitimacy and face eventual extinction.[6] Hence, judgments about organizational effectiveness are judgments about the degree to which the distribution of the satisfaction of preferences fits actual constituent preferences for performance over time. Each model of organizational effectiveness addresses the question of the distribution of the satisfaction of constituent preferences in a different manner. It is in the way in which they tackle "organizational effectiveness as a wicked problem" that they leave something to be desired.

Goal-based approaches are used most often in performance evaluation. By far, the majority of goal-based evaluations employ a managerial meta criterion in that they focus on organizational goals as defined by the organization's managers. This creates a number of problems. First, the goal-based approach treats questions concerning organizational effectiveness as tame problems. The question of whether an organization is performing effectively is interpreted as whether it is performing efficiently in attaining managerial goals or fulfilling managerial preferences for performance. A set of managerially defined goals exists and the evaluation focuses on determining whether these goals have been attained. The evaluative information provided to decision makers is directed toward the fulfillment of these managerially defined goals. If performance has attained these goals, the organization is performing effectively. If these goals have not been attained, the recommendations or action concern alternatives for attaining them. In other words, the question of what is effective performance is seen as one of finding the correct or the most efficient path for fulfilling managerial preferences.

Questions concerning the distribution of satisfactions of constituent preferences are not considered. Given the logic of the model, constituent preferences are not important. This creates a problem in that it is the public, concretely represented by organizational constituencies, which legitimizes an organization's existence. If an organization is not fulfilling its constituents' preferences, it has no reason to exist. As noted earlier, organizations are social creations designed to attain ends which would be impossible or difficult to attain through individual action. Participants will continue to be involved only as long as their prefer-

6. Pragmatically, this doesn't mean that *all* constituent preferences must be satisfied, *all* the time, a clearly impossible task. What it does mean is that an organization has to satisfy constituent preferences for performance to at least a minimal level, as defined by the constituents, over time. Given that most constituents are not sensitive to short run changes in the quality of performance as related to their preferences (Hirschman, 1972), organizations have considerable leeway in deciding when to satisfy whose preferences.

ences for performance are being satisfied to some degree.

The lack of attention to constituent preferences in goal-based models creates a difficult situation for organizational decision makers guiding an organization through its social and political environments. These evaluations of performance may show that the organization is performing effectively while, at the same time, it may be under attack from many quarters for performing ineffectively. The decision maker, trying to remedy the situation, will use available evaluative information to correct deficiencies in performance. The problem lies in the fact that the causes or dimensions of performance which have constituents judging an organization as performing ineffectively are not represented in the information the decision maker is attempting to use. In fact, actions which are recommended from goal-based evaluations may aggravate problems that an organization is encountering, because they direct the decision maker to make the organization perform more efficiently along dimensions of performance which the constituencies are complaining about. The point here is that goal-based evaluations can foster a decline in public confidence and a loss of social legitimacy because they recommend that decision makers make organizational performance more efficiently ineffective.

This may not be the case when preferences for performance are stable. But whenever the environment of an organization is changing, goal-based evaluations of performance are inappropriate since they do not reflect changing conditions which the organization must face. It will be shown in the following chapter that changing preferences for performance are the rule rather than the exception. In such situations, employing goal-based evaluations to assess effectiveness as opposed to efficiency can be hazardous to an organization's health.

Systems approaches to organizational effectiveness are prone to the same types of problems. Systems models treat organizational effectiveness as a tame problem. They view organizational performance within the context of how well, or how efficiently, an organization is attaining resources from the environment, transforming these resources, and returning the outcome of the transformation process back to the environment. The preferences of constituents, including those of managers, are not represented in the evaluative process. The problem is similar to the one noted above but more severe. Changes in managerial preferences may be represented in the goal-based evaluations. These changes may better map constituent preferences for performance, giving the goal-based evaluation a better representation of organizational reality. Systems approaches, on the other hand, provide no information about any preferences for performance. They merely examine the efficiency of organizational processes. Evaluative information counsels decision makers on how to perform more efficiently. The question is, "More efficiently doing what?" The obvious answer is to do more efficiently what you have been doing in the past. As with the goal-based approach, this will not reflect qualitative changes in constituent preferences. Hence, an organization may attempt to do more efficiently those things which are leading to declining public confidence and a loss of legitimacy. In short, treating wicked problems as though they were tame creates even more wicked problems which managers have to deal with in the future.

The multiple constituency approach, as an empirical technique, does not suffer from the same types of problems inherent in the goal-based and systems approaches. Since the approach takes constituent preferences into account, it provides a much better mapping of the decisional environment managers face. The problem lies in the meta criteria the models employ. The relativistic version of the multiple constituency model treats the approach as a simple empirical technique. It is, from a relativistic perspective, a method which is to be used providing decision makers with information on constituent judgments of performance. The problem with the relativistic perspective is that evaluators have to make a number of judgments in the evaluative process. One major judgment is deciding what constituencies are to be included in the evaluative process. The selection of constituencies will have a major effect on the outcome of the evaluation. This judgment is particularly critical since, as Rittel and Weber noted, there is no inherent stopping point for evaluative problems. Given constraints of time and money, evaluators are unlikely to have an opportunity to examine all constitutent groups' judgments of performance, especially in the case of large organizations having large numbers of constituencies. How are the relevant constituencies to be selected? It is a judgment which has to be made by the evaluator. The danger inherent in the relativistic approach is that the values or preferences of the evaluator which guide this selection are submerged. A similar problem is inherent in the nature of the evaluative information provided to organizational decision makers by the evaluator. A decision has to be made about what information is important and what isn't. Again, this is a matter of judgment guided by the evaluator's values and preferences. By assuming the cloak of relativity, the value element of the evaluative process is submerged.

Lastly, evaluators cannot ignore the implications of their actions. Managers hire evaluators to assist them in making "tough" decisions about whose preferences for performance are going to be satisfied, even if it is no more than expecting the evaluative information to justify decisions and actions already taken. Theoretically, the relativistic evaluator is precluded from playing such a role because the logic of the relativistic meta criterion specifies that any one constituent's preferences for performance and judgment of effectiveness is as good as any other. There is no way to choose between them. Although this may be the case in theory, it is unlikely that an evaluator would be so reticent in practice. The problem that arises is that the perspective of the evaluator, which is hidden from examination, is the basis for making any such recommendations or suggesting alternatives. Instead of clarifying evaluative situations by uncovering preferences for performance, the relativistic evaluator simply increases the confusion by adding another set of hidden assumptions to the evaluative process.

The social justice and power meta criteria versions of the multiple constituency approach do not create the type of problem inherent in the relativistic model. Both models approach the question of the effectiveness of performance from distinct points of view. The value orientations of the models are clear and open for examination. The problem inherent in these two models is similar to that encountered in the "whose values" dilemma discussed earlier. Consider the case of two evaluators, each employing one of the approaches, who have been retained to assess the performance of the same organization. The first step in the evaluative process that each evaluator would have to undertake is the selection of constituencies to be included in the evaluation. The evaluator employing a power meta criterion will focus on the most powerful constituencies of the organization while the social justice evaluator will pay more attention to the least advantaged constituencies. Thus, the starting point for each evaluation of performance is likely to be somewhat different. Each evaluator will assess the degree to which the selected constituencies judge organizational performance as being effective in accordance with the logic of the multiple constituency approach. If they are thorough evaluators, each will proceed to uncover the preferences for performance on which these judgments were based. Given the evaluative information each evaluator has assembled, they will construct reports accompanied with their recommendations for future managerial action.

The evaluative reports are delivered to organizational decision makers who discover that the two evaluations of performance are very dissimilar. While there is some overlap in the constituencies referred to in the two reports, each covers and emphasizes different ones. The power meta criterion evaluator emphasized the evaluations of the most powerful constituencies while the social justice evaluator emphasized those of the least advantaged. Given that the recommendations for managerial action follow from the logic of the evaluative approach, the decision makers find that the recommendations made by the two evaluators are significantly dissimilar. In fact, given the nature of the two meta criteria in question, the recommendations are likely to be diametrically opposed. One set of recommendations says serve the interests of the most powerful, the other, serve the interests of the least powerful.

While either of these sets of recommendations may be correct in terms of improving organizational performance in a given situation, neither is likely to be correct in all situations. The problem that the decision maker is faced with is which is better in this particular situation. Neither of the evaluative models provides decision makers with an indication of how to decide which serves the interests of the organization and its constituencies in the relatively best fashion. Hence, the problem with the social justice and power meta criteria lies in the way in which they formulate the nature of the wicked problem of effectiveness. Both approach the evaluative question from a predetermined perspective. Each model formulates the evaluative problem and the solution to it in terms of the underlying logic of its meta criterion. The problem is that they prematurely define (and solve) the question of organizational effectiveness and treat all evaluative situations as if they were the same. In doing so, both models ignore the context in which performance has and is taking place. While recommendations which come from these models may assist decision makers in devising "better" solutions to the problem of satisfying constituent preferences, it is unlikely that they will provide "better" solutions to all evaluative situations, because of differences in the context in which performance occurs.

An alternative perspective which overcomes most of the problems in the models cited above would treat evaluative research as an "argumentative process in the course of which an image of the problem and of the solution emerges gradually among the participants, as a product of incessant judgment, subject to critical argument" (Rittel and Weber, 1973: 162). In order to function as such, the evaluative model would need to take into account both constituent preferences for performance and the context in which performance has taken and is taking place. The evaluative model should also be sensitive to changes in preferences and context over time, particularly since performance takes place in a dynamic environment. The meta criterion of such a model would need to acknowledge the legitimacy of constituent preferences, but at the same time, not rely on constituent preferences alone to guide decisions about modifying performance. In essence, the evaluative model needs a meta criterion which treats constituent preferences for performance within the context in which performance takes place since both are important in determining the degree to which it is "good" or "bad," "better or worse," and so on.

The following chapter develops a multiple constituency model of organizational effectiveness which is designed to meet these constraints. The model, based on a social evolutionary perspective, employs an evolutionary meta criterion. This meta criterion acknowledges the role of constituent judgments of performance but also take into account the context in which performance occurs. This involves a fundamentally different manner of viewing organizations and their environments, constituent judgments of performance, and the context in which performance takes place.

3
An Evolutionary Model
of Organizational Effectiveness

Human history is the story of social evolution. It is a story of continual change which human society has experienced. Civilizations rise and fall. Governments and political ideologies come and go. Technological shifts occur. In short, society evolves. Social evolution sometimes proceeds at a very slow pace as in Europe during the Middle Ages. At other times, such as the present, social change is very rapid. Regardless of its pace, change is the rule rather than the exception.

The fact of societal change has a major implication for organizations and the assessment of organizational effectiveness. What is likely to be effective performance at one time is likely to be ineffective at another because the social context in which performance occurs changes. Organizational effectiveness is situation-specific. The definition of what is effective performance changes as the context in which performance occurs changes. The key question is: How can an organization perform effectively over the long run if the social context in which it operates is continually changing?

This chapter presents an alternative model for dealing with organizational effectiveness when viewed as a wicked problem. The model places organizational effectiveness and evaluation in an evolutionary framework. The approach centers on the unique dynamics of every organization's performance. Three distinct elements and their interactions are considered: 1) the role of constituent preferences in defining the preferred direction of social evolution; 2) how constraints create niches within which organizations exist; and 3) the effect of time on organizational performance.

Evolutionary Processes

Biological and social evolution function in much the same manner. Both are processes by which biological and social organisms fill empty niches within an ecosystem. The concept of niches is important since it is the key to explaining evolutionary change. Niches are the interstices of elementary conditions in the environment whether they are physical, biological, or social. The interaction of physical, biological, and social conditions creates the potential for biological and social forms to exist. As Boulding (1978: 12) noted, "Any ecosystem will have empty niches; that is, a potential species which would have a positive population in the system. Biological and social evolution consist mainly in the filling of empty niches through mutation." Conversely, the interaction of these conditions sets limits of what is possible in terms of performance at any given point in time. Specific biological and social forms will evolve only if conditions exist which allow their appearance and survival. Take the case of a common human artifact, the automobile. The automobile could not have evolved as a form of transportation without its precursors. The invention of the automobile grew from earlier knowledge about non-mechanized transportation, the iron and steel industry, the infant petroleum industry, and so on. Their existence made the invention of the automobile possible.

Another important characteristic of niches is their carrying capacity. Evolutionary potentials created as niches evolve from changing physical, biological, and/or social conditions. Something *can* happen. If this potential is realized fully, an evolutionary equilibrium is attained. A niche is filled to capacity. The carrying capacity of a niche is finite. In the biosphere the carrying capacity of a niche is often bounded by the availability of food. Deer populations, for example, often grow to a point which exceeds the carrying capacity of their niche. When this occurs, members of the population rapidly die off. Food supplies then become more plentiful for the remaining members of the species who reproduce and repopulate the niche. The process is essentially cyclical, with the size of a population varying around the equilibrium point.

The carrying capacity of a niche changes over time as the conditions which interacted to create the niche change. Take the case of automobiles again. The conditions resulting in the rapid development of the automotive industry in the United States began to change during the 1970s. The era of cheap energy, a major condition for the auto industry's rapid evolvement, came to an end. Changes in the availability and price of petroleum created a new set of conditions for the auto industry. The carrying capacity of the niche for large gas-guzzling vehicles was sharply narrowed.

In short, niches are the confluence of conditions which allow something to happen in terms of evolution. Niches create evolutionary potentials which may or may not be fulfilled. As the conditions which created a particular niche change, the niche itself may be modified or closed. The conditions which create a niche and a particular evolutionary potential also provide boundaries as to what is possible at any given time. While conditions may arise which allow the evolution of a biological or social form, they also define the limits of growth that those forms can take. The constant process of changing physical, biological, and social conditions creates the backdrop against which evolution occurs.

The evolutionary pattern consists of three processes: variation, selection, and retention. Variation refers to the generation of mutations within a system. Selection processes are the mechanisms through which some mutations are selected into a biological or social population. Retention refers to the process by which selected variations are retained in the larger system. While the general evolutionary pattern is the same for biological and social systems, the specific forms that these processes take are not.

Biological evolution accomplishes its niche-filling activity by acting on the genetic material of a species. Random genetic mutations create variations within a population. Through the process of natural selection, some variations are selected into the genetic pool while others are not. Natural selection is the process by which variations adaptive to new or modified ecological niches survive while relatively less adaptive mutations and organisms do not. As ecological niches evolve, organisms which were adaptive in one set of environmental conditions may no longer be so in another. Organisms which do not evolve to meet changing environmental conditions face extinction. They may or may not be replaced by organisms or species displaying more adaptive characteristics to a particular niche. Adaptive mutations are retained through the addition of their genetic information into the genetic pool of the species.

The fundamental difference between social and biological evolution is that societies do not have an encodable genetic structure. The "genetic material" of society takes a different form. Boulding (1978: 122) described it as follows:

Just as there is the genosphere or genetic knowledge in the biosphere, so there is a noosphere of human knowledge and know-how in the socio-sphere. The noosphere is the totality of the cognitive content, including values of all human nervous systems, plus the prosthetic devices by which this system is extended and integrated in the form of libraries, computers, telephones, post offices, and so on.

Hence, the noosphere is analogous to the genosphere of biological species. It is the accumulation of knowledge and culture from which human societies are constructed, and it is within the noogenetic structure of society that social evolution occurs.

Variations in social evolution take place in the form of invention and discovery. Both represent extensions or novel recombinations of existing elements of the noosphere which result in the appearance of new social forms, technologies, and human artifacts. Technological development, for example, tends to be a cumulative process. It builds upon itself, as witnessed by the exponential increase in the development of new technologies since World War II. Most progress is the result of past discovery and invention paving the way for future development. Advances in electronics brought about the advent of the computer age during the 1940s. Research building upon these earlier advances led to further developments. Today, much advanced electronic and computer design work is being done by earlier generation computers. More rare are the novel discoveries and inventions such as nuclear technology and genetic engineering. The point is that each advance, each addition to the human store of knowledge, makes even more possible by opening up new opportunities.

As variations are generated within the noosphere, selection processes come into play. Some social evolutionary selection processes parallel those of natural selection in the biosphere. Whole social forms, for instance, may evolve and survive through adaptation to changes in environmental conditions. Other selection processes, related to learning, are specific to social evolution.[7] Adaptive behaviors may, for example, evolve through imitation, learning by one individual from other individuals. Group members may promote individuals who display highly adaptive behaviors into positions of authority. Adaptive behaviors or characteristics may be learned and retained in the noosphere.

7. They had been suggested as playing a role in biological evolution by an early evolutionary theorist, Jean Baptiste Lamarck (1744-1829). Lamarck argued that biological organisms inherited acquired or learned characteristics from their parents. An organism would perceive an environmental change, respond in an appropriate way, and genetically pass the appropriate reaction along to its offspring. Although Lamarckism has been replaced by Darwinism, the notion of the inheritance of acquired characteristics plays a role in social evolution.

Selection mechanisms which are truly peculiar to social evolution are rational selection processes such as evaluation, planning, and forecasting (Campbell, 1965; 1974). These selection mechanisms have an important impact on social evolution. As Boulding (1978: 22) noted, "Human evaluations . . . have strong non-random elements in them in which orderly patterns can be perceived. Once human evaluations appear on the evolutionary scene, a whole new selective process appears in the world and the evolutionary process is markedly changed by it." These selection mechanisms are expressions of human values. Variations which are perceived as desirable are retained regardless of their adaptiveness to changing environmental conditions. Human societies, through rational selection, create their own future. This is perhaps the most striking difference between biological and social evolution. Biological organisms evolve in concert with changing environmental conditions; human societies attempt to create their own future by controlling their evolutionary path. As Boulding (1978: 136) wrote, "Whereas prehuman organisms occupy niches and expand to fill them, the human organism is a niche-expander creating the niches into which it will expand."

As a rational selection mechanism, evaluations of performance and determinations of effectiveness play an important role in guiding future organizational action in two ways. First, evaluations provide the information necessary to make determinations of the desirability of an activity. On the basis of evaluative information, decisions are made on whether to select an activity into the system's repertoire (i.e., retain it in the noosphere). Second, evaluations act as a control device by providing feedback on the performance of new or ongoing activities. Adjustments are made in organizational performance on the basis of this information with the intent of making performance more adaptive in a social system context.

Requisite Variety and Variety Matching

Rational selection mechanisms function as control devices in social evolution. It is important, therefore, that they be designed to increase the likelihood that adaptive variations are selected into the system's repertoire. The literature on cybernetics provides a number of insights into the design and operation of control devices which can be applied to evaluative research as a selection mechanism in social evolution. A major principle of cybernetics is the "Law of Requisite Variety" (Ashby, 1956), which states that control devices must have as much variety as exists in the system being controlled in order for the device to accurately register information about states of the system and perform its controlling function. Variety is defined as the number of distinguishable elements within a system being controlled.

A controlled system is composed of disturbances, essential variables, and a control mechanism. A disturbance is an environmental event (variation) which can modify an essential variable. Essential variables are the critical elements of the system being controlled. They have acceptable ranges of allowed deviation which are the parameters of system survival. If these parameters are exceeded the system will fail or be destroyed. Temperature, for example, is an essential variable of the human body. If the body's temperature exceeds a specified range, the human organism will die. The control mechanism buffers the essential variables from disturbances so that the parameters of survival are not violated. Ashby (1956) argued that for a control device to buffer the essential variables it has to have as much variety within it as exists within the disturbance. In other words, the device has to be able to distinguish between different states of a disturbance in order to counter its impact and adequately buffer the essential variable. If the control mechanism does not contain as much variety as the disturbance, it does not misinterpret or miscode the information. It simply does not register it. A couple of examples will help clarify this point.

Kirk (1978) noted that the Eskimo language has more than twenty different words for snow, while the English language has only one. The Eskimo language contains more variety within it with regard to snow than does the English language. Eskimos see at least twenty conceptually distinct forms of snow while persons speaking English see only one. While the same physical phenomenon is observed in both cases, less conceptual information is registered in English because it has less variety than Eskimo. Similarly, the eye of a frog distinguishes only four categories of events, through what are described as sustained contrast, moving edge, net dimming, and net convexity detectors (Lettvin et al., 1965). The first provides the frog with a general outline of its environment, the second registers sudden moving shadows like birds of prey, and the third responds to a sudden decrease of light as a result of such shadows. The fourth, the net convexity detector, is the mechanism which enables a frog to catch its food. It responds to small, dark, moving objects, like flies, that come into the frog's field of vision. The frog's visual system simply does not register any other information from the visual environment. Compared to the human ocular system, the frog does not have nearly as much variety in its visual system and cannot distinguish as many distinct conceptual elements in the visual environment as can the human. Human vision in turn, is also limited. The human ocular system responds to only a small segment of the electromagnetic spectrum (Ornstein, 1972). Although the variety within this system is greater than that of the frog's, it is less than the total variety in the environment. In both examples information is not misinterpreted or miscoded. It simply is not registered because the English language and the frog's eye have less variety within them than exists in the Eskimo language and in the electromagnetic spectrum.

Emery (1969) noted that the pattern of variety detected by a control device is as important as the amount of variety it detects. The pattern of variety refers to the structure of the match between variety in the system and variety perceived by the control device. Figure 3-1 presents four possible types of matches between variety within a system and variety perceived by a control device. Each of the squares represents the system while the partitioned sections represent the elements of variety within the system. In the first box, the variety of the control device matches that of the system. There are three elements of variety in the system which are accurately perceived by the control device. Both the pattern and amount of variety has been matched. In the second box, the variety perceived by the regulator is too fine in that it perceives six elements while three actually exist. In the third box, two elements of variety are perceived where there are three in the system. The control device's information structure is too coarse in that it does not distinguish between two of the elements. In the fourth box, the perception of variety is both too fine and too coarse. The regulator perceives more elements of variety than exist in the system and, at the same time, does not match the elements that do exist. In order for a control device to accurately distinguish among different states of a system, it has to match both the amount and pattern of variety in the system.

Constituent Preferences and Variety

The concept of variety can be applied to evaluative research with two modifications. First, variety within an evaluative context is not defined as states of a disturbance within a system. The major elements of variety are constituent preferences for performance. Constituent preferences determine the criteria against which performance will be assessed and effectiveness judged. As such, they are the major elements of variety which have to be taken into account if the evaluation is to provide an accurate portrayal of the state of the evaluated system. Second, the nature of the essential variables within an evaluative system

Figure 3-1

Alternate Patterns of Variety Matching

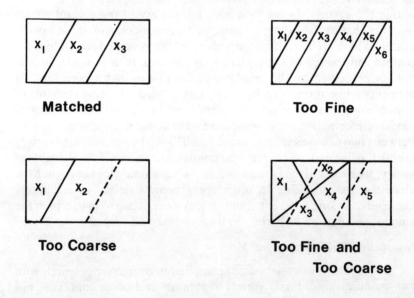

Matched

Too Fine

Too Coarse

Too Fine and
Too Coarse

is different than those of physical and biological systems. In physical and biological systems, essential variables and their parameters define the physical limits of a system. In evaluative systems, the essential variables and their parameters are socially defined by the organization's constituencies. An organization, for example, does not select job satisfaction as an essential variable. Its employees do. Similarly, customer service as an essential variable is something imposed on it by its customers. The point is that essential variables in an evaluative system are defined and imposed on organizations by their constituencies. With these modifications, the Law of Requisite Variety can be applied to evaluative research as follows: The better the match between constituent preferences for performance incorporated into an evaluation and actual constituent preferences, the greater the likelihood of adaptive actions being taken as a result of the evaluative information.

It is essential to understand that the incorporation of various constituent preferences for performance substantially complicates the life of organizational decision makers. Different constituencies will judge different aspects of organizational performance. The dimensions of performance selected and evaluated by one constituency may be inconsistent or contradict those chosen by other constituencies. Friedlander and Pickle's (1967) study of the effectiveness of ninety-seven small business firms in Texas provides an excellent illustration of this point.

Their study begins with the assumption that firms are engaged in exchange relationships with different segments of their environment and that the degree to which these relationships are satisfied is vital to organizational stability and growth. The seven organization-constituent relationships studied were: owner(s), employees, customers, suppliers, creditors, local communities, and government agencies. Sets of criteria reflecting the preferences of each constituency were developed by Friedlander and Pickle. Generally, the criteria for the creditor, supplier, owner, and government constituencies focused on the financial aspects of their relationship with the organizations. Consumer criteria centered on the service or product supplied by the firms. Local communities were concerned with the organizations' participation in community life. The employee criteria predictably involved such items as satisfaction with working conditions, financial rewards, the job itself, and personal development. The important point is that the criteria for each constituent group were plausible interpretations of the expectations or desires of each constituency. A listing of criteria by constituency is provided in Table 3-1.

Table 3-1. Criteria Used in Friedlander and Pickle's (1967) Effectiveness Study

Community
Membership/leadership in local and nonlocal organizations.
Number of committees and drives that managers participated in during two years prior to the study.
Attendance at community fairs (fund raising dinners, bazaars, etc.).

Government
Questioning about taxes by the IRS.
Penalties on state, local, and federal taxes.
Reprimands or censure from tax officials.

Customers
Quality of goods and services.
Quantity of goods and services available.
Neatness, cleanliness, and uniformity of product's appearance.
Management's knowledge of the product or service.
Speed of service.
Dependability of the business.
Rank of this business in relation to others in its field.
Helpfulness, friendliness, and appearance of the employees.

Suppliers
Promptness of payment.
Fairness in transaction.
Receptiveness to suggestions.
Overall evaluation as a customer.

Creditors
Statistical data.

Owner
Average yearly profit over previous ten years.
Average yearly profit as a function of the hours/week that the owner worked for the organization.

Employee
Satisfaction with working conditions.
Satisfaction with financial rewards.
Confidence in management.
Opinion of immediate supervisor.
Satisfaction with self-development.

SOURCE: Friedlander, F. and Pickle, H. "Components of Effectiveness in Small Organizations," *Administrative Science Quarterly, 13* (1967): 289-304. Reprinted by permission of the publisher.

Each set of criteria was summarized in the form of a scale representing each group's judgment of organizational effectiveness. The intercorrelations of the judgments of effectiveness, reproduced in Table 3-2, showed that there was a relatively low degree of convergence between the constituent judgments. Only seven of the twenty-one correlations were significant, the highest (.37) being that between satisfaction of the owner's and customer's preferences for performance. The results illustrate the fact that different constituent groups focus on different aspects of performance in arriving at judgments of effectiveness. These different sets of criteria may or may not be related to each other and there is a distinct likelihood that some of the preferences will be negatively as well as positively related.

Table 3-2. Intercorrelations of the Satisfaction of Constituent Preferences for Ninety-Seven Business Firms*

	Com-munity	Govern-ment	Satisfaction of: Customer	Supplier	Creditor	Employee
Owner satisfaction	.23*	−.12	.37†	.14	.00	.23*
Community satisfaction		.16	.04	.16	.14	.22*
Government satisfaction			−.09	.11	.20*	−.07
Customer satisfaction				.17	.23*	.23*
Supplier satisfaction					.08	.17
Creditor satisfaction						.08

*p<.05
†p<.01

SOURCE: Pickle, H. and Friedlander, F. "Seven Societal Criteria of Organizational Success," *Personnel Psychology, 20* (1967): 165-178. Reprinted, with adaptations, by permission of the publisher.

The conclusion that can be drawn from this study is that constituencies only view and evaluate those aspects of performance which affect them. In order to gain an overall assessment, performance must be examined from the perspectives of the organization's multiple constituencies since each provides only a partial evaluation of total organizational performance. This can be more formally stated in terms of the principle of complementarity (Blackburn, 1971). The principle of complementarity states that no single theory provides a complete description of a phenomenon. Correct understanding requires the application of a number of complementary descriptions. Complementary theories perceive the phenomenon in conflicting ways and logically describe it in accordance with the manner in which they perceive it. They are not independent, since they refer to the same phenomenon, but they can not be subsumed into each other. Perhaps most important is that no complementary theory of a phenomenon is complete in itself. Full description is achieved only when all the complementary theories are considered together.

In short, different constituents of an organization provide partial and complementary descriptions of organizational performance. Each constituency views performance in terms of the nature of its relationship with the organization. Since each constituency's relationship with the organization is different, all the constituent perspectives contribute unique information on organizational performance. Thus, it is only when all the constituent perspectives are incorporated into the evaluation of performance that the evaluation has sufficient variety within it to gauge the degree to which it is satisfying constituent preferences. The better the match between the variety of the evaluative mechanism and that of the system being evaluated, the greater the likelihood that adaptive decisions about performance will be made.

Although constituent preferences for performance may be loosely related, as shown in Friedlander and Pickle's (1967) study, their satisfaction by organizational performance has some important implications for the organization. As was noted earlier, the actions constituencies take with regard to their participation in the organization are based on their evaluations of its performance. If stockholders, employees, or any other constituency is dissatisfied with performance, there can be any number of dysfunctional consequences for the organization. The constituencies may stop interacting with the organization (e.g., stockholders selling their stock, employees leaving the firm, customers not buying the organization's products or services). The constituencies may impose their demands on the organization (e.g., through government regulation, consumer boycotts, shareholder resolutions). Or, they may change the quality of their interaction with the organization (e.g., employees reducing the amount or quality of their work, customers only buying certain products of the firm and not others). In order for an organization to ensure that it is meeting the demands of its constituencies it has to know what criteria they are using to judge performance. The criteria with which the constituencies judge performance will not be registered by an organization unless the organization's evaluative mechanism incorporates and captures their perspectives. Lack of variety in the evaluative mechanism reduces the likelihood of an organization making adaptive responses to constituent demands.

Constraints and Niches

While constituent preferences are important because they define the preferred state of social existence for an organization, they are insufficient for evaluation since they do not reflect what is possible in terms of performance. Consideration of environmental constraints is also important in the evaluative format because they define the limits of performance. As parameters of what is possible, constraints construct the niche in which an organization is operating. They are the boundaries of an organization's niche and, as such, the parameters of organizational performance.

Constraints take many forms. They can be physical, biological, or social. Physical constraints are generally related to the physical limits of organizational performance. The availability of materials, energy, and so on, places physical limits on the extent to which an organization can perform in a particular manner. The automotive industry, for example, could meet the demand for less polluting autos much more easily if it were not constrained by the price and availability of energy and the scarcity of materials used to build pollution control devices. Physical constraints limit what an organization can do.

Social constraints can be divided into two categories, technology and tradition. Technology is a social constraint because it is part of the body of social knowledge. The automotive industry is partially constrained in its search for ways to control automotive pollution since the control technologies are not fully developed. Presently, the automakers are committed to a catalytic converter technology which runs into the physical constraint of the availability of certain metals and the effect of the converters on energy consumption requirements. In effect, technology limits what an organization knows how to do.

The other primary form of social constraint is limits to acceptable behavior in society. These constraints can be informally or formally imposed on organizations. Informal social constraints are defined by tradition, reflected in customary practice. They are the unwritten rules of society. The boundaries of ethical business behavior, for example, are only loosely prescribed under law. Socially acceptable behavior usually falls short of what is illegal behavior. These types of constraints come from public expectations on how managers should behave. If informal constraints imposed by the expectations of society on behavior are not adhered to by organizations, they are often formalized through government regulation. Through regulation the public officially specifies minimum acceptable behavior and provides penalties for violation of minimum standards.

Biological constraints are limits placed on performance by characteristics of the biosphere. Certain design factors in the automotive industry are set because the automobile is constructed for human use. Absolute minimum size, for example, is biologically constrained. Other characteristics of biological organisms can also constrain performance. The reaction of the human body to certain chemicals (e.g., carcinogens) limits their use in industry. Or, the production of products can be constrained because of biological factors. Consider the experience of Proctor and Gamble and its product, Rely tampons. Proctor and Gamble had hoped to capture a large segment of the personal hygiene market with the introduction of its super absorbent tampon, Rely. After the introduction of the product, epidemiologists noticed an increase in the occurrence of toxic shock syndrome (TSS), a sometime fatal illness which primarily affected women. Studies suggested that the incidence of TSS was associated with tampon usage, particularly of those of the high absorbency variety. The major product in this area was Proctor and Gamble's Rely. Following the release of preliminary research findings and the ensuing adverse publicity about Rely, Proctor and Gamble withdrew the product from the market. Medical researchers are now speculating that the increased incidence of TSS was caused by the emergence of a new strain of staphylococcus bacteria which thrived in the environment created by super absorbent tampons. In effect, Proctor and Gamble's performance was constrained by a biological organism.

The niches formed by constraints are not simply a function of the constraints themselves but of their interactions across physical, biological, and social levels. While one constraint may not be critical to performance in itself, it may assume a critical position because of its interaction with other constraints. Take the example of the energy constraint which many organizations face today. On the physical level, industry is constrained by the supply and price of petroleum-based fuels and natural gas. The supply and price of these fuels interact with the limits imposed on industry by the state of technological progress. Technology acts as a constraining factor in at least two ways: 1) the alternatives to fossil fuels that are technologically feasible, such as nuclear power, are socially controversial; and 2) alternative forms of energy production, such as fusion and solar, have not been technologically perfected. The interaction of the physical constraint and the social constraints imposed by technology and acceptability creates the energy constraint which industry and the American public face today. A change in one of the interacting factors has the potential of radically changing the nature of the energy constraint. Substantial new finds of petroleum or natural gas, advances in fusion or solar technologies, or changes in the social acceptance of nuclear power could significantly alter the energy constraint.

In short, the interaction of physical, biological, and social constraints creates niches in which organizations operate to fulfill constituent preferences. The constraints which create niches define what is possible and limit the alternatives available to organizations in how they can go about satisfying constituent preferences. Thus, it is clear that examining the satisfaction of constituent preferences alone is not sufficient to gain an understanding of the effectiveness of organizational performance. Only when the niche in which an organization exists is understood will a full understanding of the impact of organizational performance on constituent preferences be gained.

The Element of Time

The final element that has to be added to the analysis of organizational performance is the dimension of time. Society evolves over time. Constituent preferences change with time, as do the niches which organizations occupy. In effect, time is a dynamic dimension within which the performance of organizations must be analyzed. Post's (1978) case study of the operations of Reserve Mining Company over a thirty year period provides an excellent illustration of the relationships among preferences, constraints, and performance within the context of time.

Reserve Mining Company began its operations in Silver Bay, Minnesota, in 1947. When it began operating, it was hailed as a corporate hero. The Silver Bay area was economically depressed because the high grade iron ore deposits in the region had been exhausted and the iron ore mining companies had pulled out. Reserve breathed new economic life into the area. It mined taconite, a low grade iron ore, which can be used as a raw material in the production of iron and steel when it is refined into taconite pellets.

Reserve's operations proceeded smoothly until the 1960s when public concern about the environment began to grow. Under an agreement with the State of Minnesota, Reserve discharged the waste product of the taconite refinement process, taconite tailings, into Lake Superior. As public environmental preferences shifted, environmentalists became concerned with the effect of the discharges on the lake's water quality. In 1970, state authorities initiated a court battle against Reserve, charging that the corporation had violated the dumping agreement and was adversely affecting Lake Superior's water quality. The object of the suit was to force the company to find another method of disposing of the tailings.

Reserve's reaction to the suit was fairly predictable. It fought the charges, claiming that the tailings were inert and were settling to the bottom of the lake. The tailings, Reserve claimed, caused no environmental damage. Part of Reserve's rationale for engaging in the court battle was that their current method of operations was very profitable (e.g., $1 million profit per month in 1973). The company was also supplying essential raw materials to its parent organizations, Armco and Republic Steel. While the suit was in progress, scientists reported finding asbestos fibers in the water supplies of cities drawing their water from Lake Superior. Taconite tailings were identical to asbestos-form fibers, a suspected carcinogenic agent. Overnight, Reserve became a corporate villain in the public eye because it was perceived as endangering the health of the populations in the three states which drew their water from the lake. Even though public furor accelerated through the mid-1970s, Reserve was able to hold off its opponents. It was not until the spring of 1980 that the courts finally forced it to discontinue its operations until it implemented a land-based method for the disposal of taconite tailings. In May, 1980, Reserve closed its operations for one week while it brought a new disposal system on line and then resumed operations.

Corporate performance did not change over the period in question but the public's judgment of effectiveness shifted radically. Reserve Mining Company mined and refined taconite ore in much the same manner that it always had. What had changed were the public's preferences for performance and the constraints under which the company operated. In 1947, environmental quality was not a salient public preference nor were there many restrictions on the disposal of taconite tailings. By the early 1970s, the public expressed a strong preference for environmental preservation and imposed strict constraints on waste disposal through the enactment of environmental protection legislation. Due to these changes, Reserve moved from the position of corporate hero to that of a corporate villain by performing in exactly the same manner over time. It is important to note that the criterion by which Reserve's management judged their operations, profit, showed it to be an effective company. The low variety corporate evaluations of performance did not register changing public preferences for performance or changes in environmental constraints. As a result, it ran afoul of the society in which it operated.

Another way to characterize these changes is in terms of the niche in which Reserve operated and the satisfaction of preferences given the constraints on performance. When Reserve began operations in the late 1940s, it satisfied the preferences of the population of the Silver Bay region by providing employment and the preferences of the parent companies through the profitable provision of raw materials. This was a niche created in part by the fact that the high grade iron ore deposits in the region were depleted. Changing environmental conditions created the niche within which Reserve could operate. Over a period of time, a new set of preferences for performance emerged, those for environmental quality. The effect of this set of preferences was the eventual imposition of environmental standards which constrained the company's operational alternatives. The niche had, in other words, changed and the performance of the company was no longer compatible with the evolving nature of its niche. New constraints required new ways of performing in order to satisfy constituent preferences.

Time is an underlying dynamic element which needs to be considered in evaluative research because preferences for and constraints on performance change over time. As preferences and constraints change, the niche in which an organization operates and the preferences which it satisfies through performance change. Organizations which perform consistently in the same manner over time and continue to evaluate performance using low variety evaluative mechanisms face the danger of becoming extinct. Given these three dimensions—preferences, constraints, and time—the question of what effective performance is within an evolutionary framework can now be considered.

An Evolutionary View of Organizational Performance and Effectiveness

The evolutionary framework requires that organizational performance be evaluated within the context of the environment in which it occurs. Instead of examining organizations and organizational performance in isolation as do other models of effectiveness, the evolutionary model counsels the evaluator to examine the organization within its environment. The distinction is subtle but extremely important. Approaching organizational assessment in this manner blurs the distinction between organization and environment. The distinction is, admittedly, arbitrary (Pfeffer and Salancik, 1978; Starbuck, 1976; Downs, 1967). It is a useful tool in some instances; but it is, as Weick (1977) noted, a mental construction imposed by individuals on their streams of experiences to make them more meaningful. The problem lies in the fact that the map is often mistaken for the territory (Bateson, 1972). This has a major dysfunctional consequence in the evaluation of organizational performance.

By separating organizations from their environment for analytical purposes, attention is directed away from the ecological effects of organizational performance. The fact that it is impossible for an organization to exist apart from its social and physical environment is usually forgotten because the organization is given a "life" of its own. It is entirely possible, within the framework of the models of organization effectiveness reviewed earlier, for an "effective" organization to damage or destroy its environment, which ultimately results in self-destruction. By redefining the unit of analysis as the organization plus environment, the conception of organizational effectiveness is expanded to a systemic level. Within this type of framework the organization does not simply adapt to the environment. Rather, the organization and the environment adapt together. The environment's problems become the organization's problems (Pondy and Mitroff, 1978).

Assessment of the functioning of organs of the human body provides a useful analogy for illustrating the idea of a systemic level of analysis. Although the organs, nerves, blood vessels, and so on of the human body are each distinctly identified, their performance is considered in relation to its impact on the whole human biological system. The liver, for example, removes toxins from the bloodstream. The question of whether removing toxins from the bloodstream is effective is moot unless the impact of the liver function is considered in the context of the whole body. Removal of toxins from the bloodstream is an essential function within the context of the whole system, without which the human organism would die. The example may seem trite since most persons know that failure of a major organ has a serious impact on the functioning of the whole organism. In discussing the performance of organ systems, the context of the impact on the whole body is assumed in the assessment of performance. The components of a system do not operate in isolation of the performance of other components in the same system.

The impact of the performance of one component on the whole system may be mediated by the performance of other components. This takes place through compensating responses by some components for lapses in performance of other components. Consider the case of an individual traveling from a low altitude to a higher altitude location. As the individual progresses upward, the amount of oxygen in the atmosphere decreases. Hence, the amount of oxygen available for absorption into the bloodstream decreases. The individual's heart will begin to race and he or she will experience a shortness of breath. The circulatory system is, in other words, compensating for the inability of the respiratory system to cope with this environmental change. Flexibility in the range of performance of the circulatory system allows it to mitigate the impact of the respiratory system's performance. Flexibility, or the ability to adapt, allows the organism to adjust to changing environmental factors.

If the individual stays at the higher altitude for a period of a few days, symptoms of physiological stress will disappear as the body acclimates to the higher altitude through a process of complex physiological changes. The human organism has adjusted to changes in the physical environment via changes in the interlocked flexible functioning of the components of the human biological system. Components of the system are buffering the whole system by modifying their performance. It is this type of interactive flexibility in performance of system components that allows the body to adjust.

The ability of a system such as the human body to adapt is limited. The greater the amount of flexibility used by the organism to meet a change, the less there is to adjust or meet other changes. In other words, adaptation precludes adaptability. Individuals who moved to a higher altitude would be less able to respond to further physiological stress than they would at a lower altitude (e.g., reduced capacity for flight or fight). The adaptation of the body to the lower oxygen content at the higher altitude reduces the ability of the human organism to adjust to other contingencies. Much the same is true of social systems. There is a finite amount of flexibility at any given point of time in the system allowing it to adapt to changing social and physical conditions. As a social system adjusts to one set of changing conditions, there remains less flexibility within it to meet other changes. This is reflected in the adage about the straw that broke the camel's back. The cumulative demands on the system determine the state or strength of the system, not each individual demand. Each demand taxes the system so that less flexibility remains to meet other demands.

Evolution is the process through which adaptability is renewed. If a group of humans moved to a higher elevation and lived there for a long period of time, individuals with a genetic predisposition toward physical characteristics amenable to high altitude living would eventually become the dominant members of the group through the process of natural selection. High altitude would be the norm for this group as opposed to their ancestors, who were genetically predisposed to lower altitudes. Those persons whose bodies functioned normally at high altitude would have more flexibility or a greater ability to adapt to changing environmental conditions than their predecessors. Hence, the biological evolutionary process increases the adaptability of the species by replacing flexibility consumed in meeting an environmental change. The selection of genetic material adaptive to environmental conditions enhances species survival.

Similarly, social evolution restores social adaptability by increasing society's ability to meet changing social and environmental conditions. Constituent preferences play two important roles in this pattern of evolution. They both denote the preferred direction of evolutionary change and create pressures on the system to change. Preferences can create pressure to change in a couple of ways. New preferences for performance which can not be satisfied within the constraints of an organization's existing niche may emerge over time. Or, changing constraints may make it difficult to satisfy existing preferences within the context of the modified niche which an organization is occupying. Changing preferences can usually be satisfied to some extent through modifications of organizational performance within an existing niche, but only at a cost. As in biological evolution, adaptation precludes adaptability. Slack which existed in the system is consumed in satisfying changing preferences, and the system has less flexibility available to meet future changes.

The Evolutionary Meta Criterion

Organizations increase the adaptability of the social system by expanding or creating new niches within which changing constituent preferences can be satisfied over time. They increase the adaptability of the system as a whole by replacing the flexibility or slack consumed in meeting demands for change. This is the crux of the difference between biological and social evolution. Biological organisms evolve to fill niches created by changing constraints. Social organisms change constraints, expanding or creating the niches which they will fill. This perspective on performance generates an alternative to the meta criteria of other models which is consistent with the evolutionary framework. The evolutionary meta criterion specifies that effective performance increases the adaptability of the organization/environment by changing the constraints on performance, allowing it to satisfy changing constituent preferences over time. The effective organization is a niche expander whose performance adds to the organization's/environment's ability to adapt to change.

It is important to keep in mind that the notion of niche expansion is relative because it refers to the relationship between organizational performance and the constraints on performance. Changes in either will result in changes in the relationship. Performance which *conserves* energy, for example, will *expand* an organization's niche under a constraint of energy scarcity as will the discovery of new sources or forms of energy. One is a change in performance, the other in a constraint. Both have the effect of expanding the organization's niche.

The evolutionary meta criterion has a number of implications for organizational action and judgments of organizational effectiveness. First, it specifies that organizational performance needs to be responsive to constituent demands. Second, it states that effectiveness stems from innovative performance which expands the noosphere, allowing organizations to satisfy changing constituent preferences. Third, "nest fouling" behavior is ineffective because the organization can not survive apart from its environment since it is part of that environment. The organization which "wins" over its environment is, in the long run, "winning" over itself because it is destroying its niche.

Take the case of industrial organizations producing steel during the 1960s and 1970s. Historically, steel was produced using a "dirty" production process which emitted considerable amounts of air and water pollutants. Pollutants from the production process had considerable physical and social costs. Physical costs were reflected in the impact of pollutants on plant and animal life and the associated degradation of the environment. Social costs included increased health care costs associated with higher incidences of disease, urban blight, and so on.

For many years, these costs of production were absorbed by the public as an "externality" of the production process. The costs were accepted as part of the price of industrial progress. But, by the 1960s, public preferences for performance began to shift toward greater awareness and concern over the impact of industry's performance on the environment. Industry as a whole did not respond to growing public concern. This resulted in the imposition of a new constraint on performance, in the form of stringent regulations governing the emission of wastes into the physical environment.

As the regulations took effect during the 1970s, a number of alternatives were open to steel producers. Some ignored the regulations or fought them in court while continuing to pollute. These orgnizations were clearly ineffective in the sense that they were failing to satisfy constituent preferences for performance through their nest fouling behavior. Their behavior imposed costs on the system which, in the final analysis, imposed costs on themselves which threatened organizational and social viability. These organizations were attempting to operate in a niche which no longer existed. The constraints on performance had changed but their behavior had not. The net effect was that they were directly jeapordizing their own existence and having a detrimental effect on the social system as a whole.

Other steel producers attempted to adjust their performance to meet the new constraints by installing pollution control devices required by government regulation. While they were meeting changed constituent preferences by reducing emissions, the companies were doing so at great cost. Diversion of resources to devise and implement emission control strategies reduced the ability of the companies to respond to future changes in preferences and constraints. Many firms were operating at the limits of their performance capability because they had adjusted to the changing preferences and constraints within the modified niche which they occupied. The organizations were performing less ineffectively than those that were continuing to pollute, but only marginally so. By adjusting performance to meet constituent preferences within the existing niche, their own adaptability was reduced because of the reduction in slack resources available to meet other changes. Similarly, the adaptability of the whole system was reduced for the same reason.

Effective performance, within the framework of the evolutionary meta criterion, required that the steel producers engage in niche expanding activities which would allow them to meet changing preferences and replace organization/environment adaptability in the process. If a steel company were, for example, to develop a nonpolluting production process for producing steel it would increase the adaptability of the organization/environment while meeting changing preferences. Creation of a new production process would remove a technological constraint on performance and expand the niche in which the companies were operating. Another alternative would have been the development of new materials produced by nonpolluting processes which could be used as substitutes for steel. In both cases, the responses would have been effective in that niche expansion would allow the firms to respond to changing preferences while increasing the viability of the organization/environment as a whole.

Both these alternatives for performance are radical departures from existing practice. They are extreme cases of effective performance and not terribly likely in the short run. What are more likely are partial departures from existing practice which modify one or more of the constraints on performance. Niche expansion can be accomplished through "small" as well as "large" actions since it is the interaction of the constraints and not the constraints alone that defines niches. The actions of Armco Steel Company illustrate how "small" innovative behaviors can be effective within an evolutionary framework through incremental deviations rather than radical departures from current practice.

During the late 1970s, engineers at Armco Steel proposed an alternative pollution control strategy to the Environmental Protection Agency (EPA), known as the "bubble concept." The bubble concept proposed that a hypothetical bubble be erected over a production facility and a standard set for the total level of emissions within the bubble, as opposed to the existing practice of setting standards for each source of emissions. Armco argued that this would stimulate innovation and efficiency in pollution control by allowing managers to trade off emissions from different sources in achieving air quality standards.

After a period of negotiation and lobbying by the steel industry, the EPA adopted a modified version of the bubble concept which allowed managers to search for trade-offs between similar pollutants. Armco was given permission to conduct a pilot project at its Middletown, Ohio, facility by applying the concept to the control of nontoxic particulates. Three types of particulates were involved: some smokestack emissions, some process emissions such as rust, and wind-blown or open dust. The strategy Armco pursued was one of stepping up efforts to control ordinary airborne dust at the facility and trade off the gains against emissions of other particulates from plant doors, windows, and vents. Armco estimated that the bubble concept would allow it to control approximately 4,000 tons of nontoxic particulates annually, compared to a reduction of 652 tons annually if the Middletown facility met the individual limits set under the conventional regulations. The estimated cost for the innovative controls was $4 million compared to $11.5 million for the controls required by conventional regulations. Overall, Armco estimated that it could save $42 million by applying the bubble concept to its other facilities while increasing air quality beyond that specified by conventional regulations.

The bubble concept increased the adaptability of the organization involved as well as the system as a whole because it restored some flexibility within the system by freeing up resources to meet other contingencies. By lowering the cost of pollution control, the bubble concept reduced the strain on the organization/environment created by the requirement that manufacturers meet changing preferences within a set niche. The innovation expanded the niche by allowing the affected companies to better meet changing preferences for performance. Better air quality was possible at less cost, freeing up resources to meet other constituent demands such as reinvestment in new plant and equipment. In short, it was effective performance in an evolutionary sense.

Wicked Problems and the Evolutionary Meta Criterion

The evolutionary model of organizational effectiveness can be compared to the others discussed in the last chapter on the basis of its treatment of effectiveness as a wicked problem. First, other models of effectiveness offer definitive formulations of effectiveness based on their meta criteria. Each specifies a correct way of looking at questions of effectiveness. The evolutionary model provides a formulation of effectiveness but not in the same sense as the others. It is not a definitive formulation. Within the evolutionary framework, there are many alternative formulations of effectiveness since there are many ways to view the satisfaction of constituent preferences in light of constraints on performance. Given that many factors constrain the performance of any organization, there are many alternative actions or strategies which could expand an organization's niche, allowing it to better satisfy preferences over time. What the evolutionary meta criterion does do is focus attention on the relationship between constituent preferences and constraints.

A second characteristic of wicked problems is that they have no stopping rules. There is no inherent logical point in viewing a wicked problem. Other models of effectiveness view evaluations as discrete events providing definitive judgments of effectiveness. The evolutionary approach, on the other hand, views evaluations as episodes of assessment. The question of what is effective performance continues through time because preferences and constraints are continually changing.

The evolutionary meta criterion does not treat solutions to problems of effectiveness as if they were true/false nor does it raise the perspective of one constituency above those of others. Effectiveness stems from the ability of an organization to satisfy changing preferences of its constituencies over time. The goal of performance is to satisfy constituent preferences, regardless of whether the constituents are powerful, disadvantaged, members of the managerial elite, etc., through the expansion of an organization's niche. The greater the degree to which an organization is able to satisfy constituent preferences for performance, the "better" its actions. Since there are many ways to accomplish the expansion of a niche, there are no true or correct solutions. Many strategies or actions can result in an organization being better able to fulfill preferences. The goodness of these solutions comes from the fact that by expanding its niche and satisfying preferences, an organization enhances its legitimacy within the social system and increases the adaptability of the organization/environment. Effectiveness is judged in relation to the actions and strategies of an organization in enhancing its viability and the larger social system's viability over time.

Unlike in other models, no single constituent perspective is raised to a position above those of other constituencies. This is to say that all the constituencies have a legitimate stake in the functioning of an organization but none has a predominant set of interests, although it may be more important to satisfy one constituency at one point in time than others. Social legitimacy and the continued participation of the constituencies depends on satisfaction of their preferences over time. In other words, the evolutionary approach does not raise the question of whose preferences should be satisfied. Rather, it's a question of how preferences are going to be satisfied.

Again, there are no immediate or ultimate tests for the solutions of wicked problems. Every solution to a wicked problem is a one-shot operation. Both these characteristics are related to the fact that solutions to wicked problems change the system. Since the system is changed, the solution can not be tested against the earlier state of the system. The earlier state no longer exists and it usually takes a long time for the impact of a solution to be felt. Organizational performance changes the niche within which an organization operates. An organization's actions contribute to shaping the future states of the system and preferences that organizations will face in the future. Other models of organizational effectiveness ignore this aspect of performance. It is inherent in the evolutionary approach because the goal of organizational performance is niche expansion which allows organizations to better fulfill preferences over time.

Since every wicked problem is unique, the assessment and judgment of organizational effectiveness is organization-specific. Every organization creates and occupies a niche somewhat different from those of other organizations, even competing organizations. The implication is that assessment of organizational effectiveness is an essentially unique activity for every organization. Assessment and understanding of the impact of performance can not be gained unless performance is viewed within the context of the particular niche within which an organization is operating. Other models of effectiveness ignore this aspect of the performance/context relationship.

The evolutionary perspective on organizational effectiveness does a better job portraying organizational effectiveness as a wicked problem than do other models in the literature. The model specifies that effectiveness is related to the satisfaction of preferences within a particular context over time through niche expanding activities which increase the adaptability of the organization/environment. As such, it provides a distinctly different orientation to the assessment of organizational performance. The following chapters present two case studies which illustrate the application of the evolutionary approach. The first case focuses on the performance of a number of small, public sector organizations known as physician extender training programs. The evaluation of these programs is initially presented from the perspective of a goal-based evaluator. The goal-based evaluation is then expanded through examination of the preferences of program constituencies for and constraints on performance. The case illustrates how low variety evaluations may blind evaluators and decision makers to problems and opportunities by not registering pertinent information about organizational performance. It also demonstrates the dynamic interactive effects of preferences and constraints over time.

The second case describes the performance of three large, private sector organizations, the Big Three automakers, during the 1970s. The case begins with the assumption that the overall performance of large organizations can not be evaluated in a formal sense. It is argued that high variety evaluative processes which provide a continuous flow of evaluative information on the impact of performance and changing preferences and constraints must be built into the decision-making structure of large organizations. The analysis focuses on the perceptions of and responses to changing preferences and constraints by the Big Three automakers. The control systems and performance of GM, Ford, and Chrysler during the period in question are examined and compared. While the physician extender case approaches constituent preferences and constraints from an evaluative standpoint, the automotive case presents the same types of information from a managerial orientation. The final chapter expands on the themes of this chapter and the two case studies and discusses the implications of the evolutionary approach for evaluative practice and strategic behavior.

4

Case One: An Evaluation of Physician Extender Training Programs

Federal programs often are created to occupy niches within the social environment that are not filled by private sector organizations. The demand for the program comes from various public constituencies or special interest groups, all clamoring for legislative attention in the U.S. Congress. Executive branch agencies implement legislative mandates formalized by Congressional action. In many instances, mandated programs are contracted to organizations outside the federal government. Such contracts usually specify that the programs be formally evaluated.

These evaluations invariably employ a goal-based approach. The logic underlying the utilization of the goal-based approach is fairly straightforward. The federal government wants to know whether it got what it paid for. The problem with this is that the goal-based approach can have a number of dysfunctional consequences for program management. Since the information provided by goal-based evaluations does not reflect changes over time, in constituent preferences or in the environmental constraints which created the niche for the programs in the first place, programs often quickly fall out of step with the purposes they were created to serve. This chapter presents a case study of the development and evaluation of federally funded programs created to train physician extenders. It illustrates the differences between the types of information decision makers receive from the goal-based and the evolutionary evaluative approaches. These differences can have a marked effect on the types of actions which decision makers select to guide present and future organizational performance.

Background

In the early 1960s, health care policy makers became concerned with the growing shortage of medical care available primarily to the poor in urban and rural areas. At the time, the demand for health care services was outstripping the supply of physicians. Medical and nursing educators formulated plans to fill this gap by considering ways to use individuals with less training than physicians in the areas of diagnosis and treatment of illness. This resulted in a proliferation of new health care roles designed to supplement physicians in providing health care services. Persons in these new roles were trained to perform some of the routine tasks traditionally associated with physician practice. These new health professionals were referred to as physician extenders.

Physician extenders were trained to conduct physical examinations, take medical histories, order and interpret diagnostic laboratory tests, order x-rays, treat specified minor and chronic illnesses, and prescribe medications for these illnesses under standing orders from supervising physicians. In some states, extenders are allowed to prescribe certain drugs over their own signatures. Extenders work with physicians and usually have treatment protocols which guide their activities. If extenders encounter conditions they are not trained to treat, they refer the patient to a physician for care. The use of physician extenders enables physicians to concentrate on patients requiring their advanced medical skills and experience.

The term physician extender includes both physician's assistants and nurse practitioners. The first physician's assistant training program, designed to train former military corpsmen, was started by Dr. Eugene Snead in 1965 at Duke University. By 1970, a number of other physician's assistant programs had been developed at such institutions as the Stanford Medical Center and the University of Washington. These programs received funding from a variety of sources, including the Veterans Administration, the Office of Economic Opportunity, the Model Cities Program, the Departments of Defense and Labor, as well as private foundations and state governments. A number of nurse practitioner programs also were developed during this period. Dr. Henry Silver at the University of Colorado, for example, trained pediatric nurse practitioners beginning in 1965.

Subsequently, Congress enacted the Comprehensive Health Manpower and Training Act of 1971 and the Nurse Training Act of 1971, which authorized the Department of Health, Education, and Welfare (HEW) to fund programs for training physician's assistants and nurse practitioners, respectively. The intent of these two laws was to improve the health delivery system and the distribution, supply, quality, use, and efficiency of health care personnel. By 1974, HEW funded approximately one hundred physician extender training programs with about $34 million. When all sources of funding are included, approximately seventy programs were training physician's assistants and two hundred fifty programs training nurse practitioners by 1977. Subject to general goals set by HEW, these programs were expected to develop training methods to fit local needs. The programs funded by HEW assumed a wide variety of training postures since no specific guidelines for training physician extenders had been developed. Given a general set of goals, programs were expected to develop training methods to fit local needs.

Program Evaluation from a Managerial Perspective

As part of the early development of the physician extender concept by HEW, the National Center for Health Services Research and Development constructed a Uniform Manpower Evaluation Protocol,

which was designed to determine, in part: methods of maintaining effective health care standards; the strengths and weaknesses surrounding the use of physician extenders as perceived by physicians, incumbents, and patients; and the impact of the extenders on the redistribution of medical services in the areas of low access. (U.S.G.A.O., 1975: 7)

HEW contracted for an evaluation of a physician's assistant training program using the protocol during 1971-3. The contractor concluded that the protocol was a meaningless evaluation tool, and an official from the National Center reported that the results of this research were virtually useless for evaluation purposes.[8]

It appears that there have been no later efforts on the part of HEW to conduct a systematic evaluation of its physician extender efforts. The contract for each training program specifies that programs are to conduct evaluations of both their training of physician extenders and their impact on the health care system. As a result, there has been a proliferation of studies on the findings of these evaluations. Although this may appear to be a haphazard way in which to evaluate a large federal program, it did lead to the appearance of a number of unique reports—evaluative studies with different foci and unusual approaches.

At the time the extender role was conceived, there was little empiri-

8. It is not ascertainable from the literature as to why this was the case.

cal evidence as to whether extenders could perform the expected tasks. The initial question faced by program administrators concerned whether or not physician extenders could perform competently. Focusing on this question, the evaluation literature soon provided ample documentation as to the ability of extenders to perform competently.[9] An exemplar of these studies was the Burlington trials conducted in Ontario, Canada. This study employed an experimental design which compared physician and nurse practitioner practice with regard to the skills acquired by nurse practitioners above and beyond their traditional nurse training. The results of this study (Sackett et al., 1974; Spitzer et al., 1974) and others (e.g., Stein, 1974; Duncan et al., 1971; Fine and Silver, 1973; Burnip et al., 1976) revealed that there were no substantial differences between physician and nurse practitioner practice in the areas in which nurse practitioners were trained to perform.

A number of studies also contain findings on the comparative treatment and control by physicians and physician extenders of specific chronic diseases, such as hypertension and diabetes. Generally, these studies revealed that physician extenders were able to detect and control specific chronic illnesses at a level of competence comparable to that of physicians (e.g., Stein, 1974; Alderman and Schoenbaum, 1975). Analyses of the tasks performed by physician extenders in a number of different health care settings have also been performed. The results of these studies have shown that physician extenders do perform the tasks they have been trained to perform once they are in a practice setting (e.g., Turner and Zammuto, 1975; Merenstein et al., 1974). Patient encounter studies examined the types of patients and conditions seen by physician extenders during the course of their practice and revealed that extenders did see the types of patients and conditions that they were trained to see (e.g., Schulman and Wood, 1972; Turner and Zammuto, 1975; Wirth et al., 1977). This body of literature shows that extenders were capable of performing in the areas, and at levels of competence, that program designers intended.

Educators also realized that acceptance of the physician extender role by patients would be critical to its success. Kissick (1968) noted that as early as 1963 it was recognized that one of the most formidable

9. The majority of evaluative studies on nurse practitioners and physician's assistants have reported similar findings. With this in mind, I have taken the liberty of referring to nurse practitioners and physician's assistants generally as physician extenders, and mixing citations. A conscious effort has been made to provide at least one reference for both types of physician extenders when the results of the studies are similar. When the findings for the two types of extenders are different or it is inappropriate to refer to the two together, it is so noted in the text.

obstacles to the downward transfer of physician functions would be consumer acceptance. Evaluative studies, however, soon indicated that patient acceptance was not a major barrier. A number of studies reported that the majority of patients seen by extenders were satisfied with the care they received (e.g., Henry, 1973; Nelson et al., 1974; Charney and Kitzman, 1975; Kahn and Wirth, 1975; Merenstein et al., 1975); and, in a number of instances, patients indicated that they would prefer seeing an extender instead of a physician. There were a number of explanations for this. Extenders often spent more time with patients than did physicians. Physician extenders, particularly nurse practitioners, received more extensive training in the psycho-social aspects of patient care and spent more time counseling and teaching patients (Dixon, 1972; Henry, 1974). Counseling and teaching have been traditional functions of nursing care and not of medical practice. Patients also may have perceived fewer differences in social status with physician extenders than with physicians and may have felt more comfortable with them. As a result, patients tended to be more open with extenders than with physicians, asked more questions, and received more information about their condition from extenders than they did from physicians. Overall, patients were usually very satisfied with the services they received from physician extenders.

The findings of these and other evaluative studies revealed that physician extenders were able to provide basic primary health care services without a diminution in the quality of these services. Program administrators and HEW concluded that the training programs had been effective. It is interesting to compare this judgment with the initial goals of the programs. Originally, physician extender training programs were created to expand the availability of primary health care services to medically underserved populations at a relatively lower cost. The findings of the studies on which judgments of effectiveness were based indicated that extenders could competently provide these services. However, there was a substantial difference between the original program goals and the evaluative information on which judgments of effectiveness were based. The stated goals of the programs and what the evaluations examined were two different things.

What occurred was an interaction between the goal-based evaluation process and the programs' goals. The goal-based evaluative approach required that programmatic goals be stated in an operative form so that they could be observed and measured. The evaluative question became: How do you train individuals to provide primary medical care services competently? Whether physician extenders could be trained to perform certain services competently was observable and measurable. Hence, program success could be judged "objectively." Doing what was measurable became synonymous with what was effective.

A 1975 report by the U.S. General Accounting Office (GAO) examined the extent to which extender training programs had attained the original program goals. The GAO findings illustrate the effect of treating a wicked problem as if it were tame. The overall findings were that the programs had not been particularly effective in expanding the availability of primary health care service for two reasons. First, extenders were trained to work with physicians and the supply of physicians was unequally distributed with regard to the health care needs of the general population. Hence, there was a structural barrier which inhibited extender programs from increasing the availability of services to medically underserved populations. Second, as was true of physicians, physician extenders tended to stay in the areas in which they were trained. Since the majority of extender training programs were affiliated with major medical and nursing education institutions, many extenders practiced in areas with a relative abundance of health care personnel and facilities. Training programs were increasing the supply of health care providers but were doing little to change their clustered distribution. The programs were, in other words, not placing the extenders in areas with the greatest needs.

The GAO report also noted that these programs were having difficulties in providing primary care services at a cost lower than that of physician-provided care. This was so because the training programs were directly constrained by the larger health care delivery system itself. State medical and nursing laws restricted the delivery of primary health care services to physicians. Extenders were, for all practical purposes, practicing medicine without a license. Physicians, nurses, and technicians had accreditation processes which legitimized their roles within the health care delivery system. Extenders did not. Consequently, third-party insurers did not recognize extenders as bona fide providers of medical care. Many health care agencies avoided this constraint by billing for extender services as if they were provided by physicians, at physician rates. Obviously, there was no reduction in the cost of care provided to patients.

Another problem with the extender training program was the difficulty of getting the role implemented within existing health care agencies. Doctors, nurses, other health care personnel, and agency administrators had serious reservations about extender practice and did not readily accept the introduction of extenders into their practice settings. As a result, many physician extenders found that they could not provide their services, however competent they were.

Each of these factors had a substantial negative impact on the ability of training programs to accomplish the goal of providing more primary health care services to medically underserved populations at a relatively lower cost. The perspectives of several constituencies on the programs' performance and the environmental constraints faced by the programs explain why they were only partially successful. Moreover, there were a number of steps that could have been taken to improve the programs and accomplish the mission. Standing in the way of such actions were the aforementioned evaluations showing that the programs were performing effectively. A problem inherent in a goal-based approach to evaluating program performance is that it places a set of blinders on program success. Commonly, the evaluations focused on the technical performance of the physician extenders. By focusing on this, the evaluators ignored a number of other equally important evaluative questions.

Studies on the technical competency of extender performance had to be conducted in settings in which the role had successfully been implemented. They could not be done where the role had not been successfully implemented. Many of these practice settings were affiliated with extender training programs. As a result, the literature reported many successes and very few failures in implementing the role. Even in those studies which were conducted in settings in which the role had been successfully implemented, there were allusions to problems in the relationships between physician extenders and other health care personnel. Little, if any, of this information was explored in evaluative studies because implementation itself, and the problems associated with it, were not a part of the evaluative focus derived from the program administrators' perspective. Program administrators, for all practical purposes, were concerned with getting competently trained extenders out the door and not with what happened to them once they left the training program. Indeed, what did happen to these people once they left the training programs was very important. The program goals could not be accomplished unless extenders could practice in their role. None of the benefits envisioned from training non-physicians to provide medical care could be realized unless they were actually providing such care.

A variety of environmental constraints also had an impact on program performance in terms of what the programs could accomplish at any particular performance. Changes in the supply and distribution of physicians, third-party insurers' policies toward extenders, etc., changed significantly from the mid-1960s to the late 1970s. These changes had a profound effect on what the programs could accomplish. The goal-based evaluations were insensitive to the context of the health care delivery system. As a result, many opportunities to improve performance were missed because administrators were not provided with evaluative information on just how the constraints affected their program performance.

The following sections trace the training program preferences and concerns of four major constituent groups: the physician extenders themselves, physicians, traditional nurses, and health care administrators.[10] Five major environmental constraints which effected the impact of training program performance are also discussed. This discussion will demonstrate the complexities involved in increasing the availability of primary health care services to medically underserved populations at a relatively lower cost. The type of evaluative information that can be provided by an evolutionary evaluative approach will also be discussed.

Other Perspectives on Program Performance

Physician Extenders[11]

Nurse practitioners start out as registered nurses who want something more out of their profession. They go into practitioner training because they want more variety and responsibility in their work. They are a self-selecting group. Most feel very positive about their new role, both personally and professionally, after training. Many found the role to be challenging. One nurse practitioner said:[12]

I find that since I am a nurse practitioner I think much differently of myself. My independence in judgment and action professionally is greatly enhanced. I *know*

10. Admittedly, this is only a small number of the constituent perspectives that could be included in an assessment of training program performance. Others that are important and which might be included are the perspectives of state and local governments, third-party insurers, Congress, other health care personnel, the professional associations of medicine and nursing, etc. As will be seen in the following, these four perspectives are the primary ones which need to be considered. They amply demonstrate the complexity of constituent preferences for performance and the impact of preferences on an organization's ability to perform.

11. The commentary in this section will focus primarily on nurse practitioners since my experience was with a nurse practitioner training program. According to Bursic (1977), the following is also representative of the feelings of physician's assistants about their role.

12. The comments from nurse practitioners in this section were obtained during a study on role implementation conducted by the author and his colleagues (Zammuto et al., 1979).

that I have much more self-respect as compared to when I was in a traditional nursing role. I feel challenged, I have a greater chance to use my professional brain.

Such feelings were common, particularly enthusiasm for the new challenge.

Nurse practitioners in health care agencies, however, had different reactions. The following comments by two practitioners were typical:

I feel very frustrated at not being allowed to function to my fullest capacity as a pediatric nurse associate. I would like very much to find a position that would allow me more freedom. . . . To date this seems almost impossible. My feeling is that the role of the pediatric nurse associate is not at all accepted by the medical community.

I have enjoyed working with Dr. ZZZZ but am frustrated because I am doing only a portion of what I feel I am capable of doing as a nurse practitioner. Dr. ZZZZ has me limited in my functions.

A nurse practitioner in one large clinic noted:

[The clinic] has very few medical nurse associates. They really don't know what to do with them, how to classify them or slot them. They're trying to fit round pegs into their square holes.

In many cases the role simply couldn't be implemented in the employing health care agencies. Nurse practitioners, asked why they left these agencies, responded:

Numerous reasons, one of which was not being allowed to function as a medical nurse associate (MNA). There was a lot of conflict between the physicians about what they wanted from an MNA.

I was never employed as a pediatric nurse associate (PNA). The year following my PNA course there was not a physician [in the agency] willing to employ me as such.

Nursing supervisors did not accept the pediatric nurse practitioner role; consequently, I could not function as a pediatric nurse practitioner despite a concentrated effort by myself and [my] preceptor.

After completing the pediatric nurse associate course, the role was never developed at the clinic and I was never allowed to practice. I was still treated as the same nurse [as] before entering the program.

Dr. ZZZZ's partner did not accept the concept of the pediatric nurse associate. The patients sensed this and I clearly saw it. He wanted me to remain, but not use my knowledge.

This was not true in all the settings. Of the one hundred forty-three nurse practitioners involved in the study from which these comments came, eighty-seven were still employed by their sponsoring agencies in the nurse practitioner role. It is important to note that twenty-six of the nurse practitioners who left their sponsoring agencies obtained employment in other agencies as nurse practitioners. A few did go back to traditional nursing.

The nurse practitioners also reported other dissatisfactions. A major complaint was the lack of understanding by other health professionals as to what the practitioners were trained to do. This often resulted in their underutilization and, in a few cases, attempts to use the practitioners as physicians. The practitioners also had some reservations about their training. Some felt they needed more than a six month training program. They enrolled in continuing education courses and several went to school to obtain advanced degrees. One enrolled in medical school.

Where the role was successfully implemented and integrated into the operation of a health care setting, a number of revisions in the beliefs and expectations of the participants (physicians, nurses, administrators, clerks, technicians, etc.) had to occur. As one respondent observed:

It was a difficult learning process for my fellow nurses, my pediatricians, the patients, and myself (not to say the other thirty-four MDs, x-ray technicians, physical therapists, pharmacists, lab technicians, and bookkeeping personnel) that had to deal with me in my new role.

The role was unsuccessful in some agencies primarily because of resistance by other health professionals. To understand the dynamics of this process, the perspectives of physicians, nurses, and agency administrators are examined.

Physicians

With regard to physician extenders, physicians were somewhat schizophrenic. In the early days of the physician extender movement, physicians' associations supported the movement. The American Medical Association, for example, formally endorsed the physician extender role and disseminated large amounts of information about it through the *Journal of the American Medical Association*. The American College of Pediatrics and the American Nurses' Association collaborated in the development of guidelines for the training and practice of pediatric nurse practitioners. Professional societies have also been active in other specialty areas.

The reaction of individual physicians outside academic medicine has been very different. Dr. Malcolm Todd, representing the American Medical Association Council on Health Manpower, said in 1973: "While many believe that there is a need and place for the physician extender, it is no secret that many doctors in the U.S.A. are vehemently opposed to this concept" (Todd, 1974:82). He went on to explain:

Physicians have expressed concern about the entire concept. Some believe that [physicians] have had little so say about the development of the physician's assistant and that the impetus has come from educators, policy makers, and the organizers of health services. In other words, the demand for the physician's assistant came from outside of the medical profession itself.

Many doctors do not know how to utilize such assistants and are reluctant to delegate tasks that they have traditionally reserved for themselves or perhaps delegated to office nurses or medical assistants. Forcing doctors to delegate tasks may be viewed as making them surrender such tasks and will not achieve the objectives sought. Moreover, the success of the physician's assistant depends as much on his relationship with the supervising physician as on where he was trained or the length or character of the programme from which he graduated. . . .

The future viability of this occupation on a national scale is largely undetermined. Many physicians have expressed concern that if physician's assistants are produced in large numbers, they may become substitute physicians. . . .

Recent surveys of selected groups of physicians have revealed that while 60 percent of those surveyed may feel the need for additional help, only 30 percent indicated an inclination to hire such additional help for their own practice if such help were available. (Todd, 1974: 79)

When the relationship between physicians and female nurse practitioners is examined, sex role conflict enters as another potent force inhibiting acceptance (Bates, 1975; Bullough, 1976; Kalisch and Kalisch, 1977).

Physicians who have worked with physician extenders are more likely to accept their role than those who have not. As noted earlier, extenders have performed competently. Furthermore, extenders foster better utilization of physician time. They tend to increase the number of patients physicians can see. Of course, some of the additional time is used by physicians away from direct patient care. In other words, they spent less time practicing medicine (Pondy et al., 1973; Lees, 1973;

Kahn and Wirth, 1975). This is cost effective since extenders cost less to train than physicians. The return on extender services (i.e., revenue from extender practice less the costs of extender practice) is greater than that for physician services, particularly if extender services are reimbursed at physician rates. The important point is that the extenders provided physicians with a scarce resource: time.

Traditional Nurses

Nurse practitioners are drawn from the ranks of traditional nursing. Many nurses resented nurse practitioners when they first entered a health care agency. One explanation for this was that the nurse now had to take orders from a former colleague. The nurse practitioners also upset the existing network of role relationships within a given practice setting. They inserted a new layer of role relations into the work process. The presence of nurse practitioners also caused traditional nurses to examine their own relationship with physicians.

Where nurses were comfortable with existing nurse-physician relationships nurse practitioners were regarded "heretics" since they were no longer bound by the strictures of the traditional nursing role. Practitioners did have more collegial relationship with physicians, ordered laboratory tests, changed medications, and instructed the other nurses to perform traditional nursing tasks. All these things could cause resentment. All these led to conflicts—with the practitioner, the agency, or with physicians at the agency.

After gaining experience with a practitioner, the situation usually improved as the role was successfully integrated into the setting's operations. Turner et al. (1973) conducted a study on the role acceptance of nurse practitioners by various categories of health professionals and found that 74 percent of the nurses in traditional roles perceived nurse practitioners as being well accepted by nurses in traditional roles. The respondents gave a number of reasons for this: (1) 41 percent saw the nurse practitioner as a role model encouraging them to continue their own education; (2) 52 percent thought that the nurse practitioner encouraged them to assert a greater degree of independence in their own practice as nurses; and (3) almost two-thirds of the nurses felt that the practitioner was a good source of information. The study also noted that, in several instances, the orientation of some nurses in traditional roles toward nursing practice caused problems and constituted the basis for conflict between nurse practitioners and nurses.

The situation with physician's assistants was probably more extreme. In 1972, the American Nurses' Association declared that "nurses do not consider it legal or ethical to take orders from physician's assistants" (*Medical World News,* 1972: 231). This situation has improved since then with the advent of legislation sanctioning physician's assistant practice and certification. In short, the reaction of traditional nursing to physician extenders has often been marked by confusion and lack of understanding of the physician extender concept. This acted as a barrier to the successful implementation of the physician extender role in many health care settings.

Agency Administrators

The response of agency administrators to the introduction of physician extenders was mixed. This was, in part, a function of the response of the other constituencies to physician extenders within the health care agency. If other constituencies did not accept the role, both the operation of the health care agency and the administrator's job were affected adversely.

Other problems associated with the introduction of a physician extender concerned agency administrators. The structural characteristics of most agencies were not amenable to the introduction of extenders. The entry of the extender typically required redesign of the flow of patients through the agency and the reallocation of resources. If these barriers were overcome, and they often were not (Zammuto et al., 1979), extenders could perform in their role and make a contribution to the agency's operation. In many cases, successful implementation resulted in better utilization of agency resources, cost savings, and a better continuity of care for patients. Other problems confronting administrators were the reimbursement policies of insurers for extender services and the legal status of the extender role. The degree to which these factors were problems varied, depending in part on the location of the agency, the type of health care setting, and the attitude of specific third-party insurers.

Based on the evaluation of physician extender programs from these four perspectives, it is apparent that the single perspective program evaluations ignored a large part of the training programs' performance and at least one major set of evaluative questions related to the implementation of the role. It is also necessary, when assessing the effectiveness of an organization's performance, to examine the context of the system in which the organization is operating. Context constantly shifts, creating new possibilities for organizational performance.

Constraints on Performance

The environmental context in which the physician extender training programs were nested is important in describing the organization's performance. It is the background against which the assessment of the organization's performance should be made. In retrospect, at least five major contextual elements constrained the performance of physician extender training programs: (1) the supply of physicians; (2) the composition of the supply of physicians and nurses; (3) state laws governing medical and nursing practice; (4) certification of extenders; and (5) third-party payment for extender services. These contextual elements were highly dynamic and interactive as the following analysis will show.

The Supply of Physicians

There was a shortage of physicians in the late 1950s and mid-1960s (U.S. Public Health Service, 1959; Fein, 1967; Carnegie Commission, 1970). This shortage provided the major impetus for training physician extenders. During the 1960s, even as the federal government experimented with extender training programs, it increased its support for medical education. This had a substantial effect on the supply of physicians. In 1967, there were 247,000 physicians providing patient care in the United States. By 1977, another 122,000 providers of primary health care had been trained. About 10 percent of these additional providers were physician extenders, the remainder were physicians. This represented a 50 percent increase in the supply of providers of primary health care in just ten years. A 1976 report by the Carnegie Council on Policy Studies in Higher Education, which in 1970 had presented an elaborate plan for the expansion of medical training, called for a moratorium on the growth of medical education. Where there had been a shortage of physician personnel in 1965, there was the growing potential of an oversupply. The effect was that the major condition which created a need for the role had, to a large degree, been alleviated.

Changing Composition of the Supply of Physicians and Nurses

Changes in the composition of the supply of physicians and nurses are related to the growth of the supply of physicians discussed above and changes in nursing education. Nursing education has been marked by a shift from three year hospital diploma training programs toward four year baccalaureate programs. This was supposed to result in better educated nurses. With more students training as physicians and nurses, the average age of physicians and nurses declined. Fellers et al. (1976) reported in a study of Illinois physicians' attitudes toward hiring physician's assistants that as the age of the physician decreased, willingness to hire a physician's assistant increased. This reflected two influences. Proportionately more physicians and nurses were entering these professions than at any other time, causing a decrease in the average age of these professionals. It also reflected a qualitative change in their training. Medical and nursing students began to receive information on the physician extender concept and its relation to their profession during the course of their professional training. As more of these newly trained physicians and nurses entered the health care delivery system, there was a general decline in resistance to the role, making it easier to implement.

Legal Status of Physician Extenders

When the physician extender movement began, the role was not sanctioned under state medical and nursing practice acts. These acts prohibited the performance of any function traditionally associated with medical practice by anyone other than a physician. Medical and nursing associations began lobbying in the late 1960s for amendments to state medical and nursing practice acts which would allow extender practice. By the summer of 1973, at least thirty-seven states had enacted physician's assistant legislation while at least twenty-eight had amended their nursing practice acts to include nurse practitioners. These statutes varied from allowing limited delegation to physician's assistants to sanctioning independent practice by nurse practitioners (Alaska, Nevada, and New Hampshire). Since then, a number of other states have enacted legislation covering physician extenders and the matter is under study in others.

This reflects one aspect of the legitimization of the physician extender role. Where in 1965 extenders were practicing medicine without a license, by 1975 the situation had changed so that over half the states recognized the extender as a legitimate provider of primary health care. Legitimization of the role also reduced barriers to implementation.

Certification

Certification was an important issue in two respects. First, many states look toward professional certification as a method for determining who is a bona fide physician extender. Second, it was a major step in the legitimization of the new role. Events surrounding the certification of nurse practitioners and physician's assistants revealed a fundamental difference between nursing and medicine over the extender role. To understand the events surrounding the certification process, the nursing profession's view of nurse practitioners must be examined. The nursing profession strongly resented the application of the term physician extender to nurse practitioners. This was based on the belief that nurses have a distinct functional role. Nursing saw nurse practitioners as complementing the physician rather as a supplement or substitute.

The difference between the professions over the definition of the physician extender role has been reflected in accreditation. In the early 1970s, the National Commission for the Certification of Physician's Assistants, which represented the major medical societies and associations, laid the groundwork for a national certification examination for physician's assistants. As a result, the National Board of Medical Examiners developed the Certifying Examination for Assistants to the Primary Care Physician, which was first administered in December, 1973. The American Nurses' Association took the following position on this certifying examination:

The certification process for physician's assistants is not designed for nurses and . . . nurses will not be encouraged, invited, or coerced into participation in the certification process including setting [sic] for taking the examination. It is recognized that some nurse might select the routes of a Certified Physician's Assistant; however, the implications for scope and practice as it relates to the state's medical and nursing practice acts remains to be tested, perhaps in the courts. (U.S.G.A.O., 1975: 19)

Evidently, this statement was effective in dissuading most practitioners from taking the exam. Only 10 percent of those eligible were present. By the end of 1977, the nursing profession had put its own certification process into action.

Given that the certification mechanisms are now in place, the question becomes one of whether the states and health insurers will accept certification as the basis for determining who is a bona fide physician extender.

Third-Party Payment

A fifth major constraint were the policies of health care insurers concerning reimbursement for extender-provided service. Third-party payment plays an important role in health care. Morris (1977) noted that in fiscal 1974, for example, 65 percent of all health care expenses were paid by third-party insurers while the remaining 35 percent were covered by direct payments from individuals. Health insurance is the major financial vehicle for the payment of health care expenses.

It is obvious that the policies of health insurers had an effect on the practice of physician extenders. Most health insurers do not recognize physician extenders as bona fide providers of medical care. This included the Supplemental Medical Insurance provisions of the Medicare program (Part B). Medicaid, a joint federal-state health insurance program for the indigent, reimbursed for extender services in some states and not in others. While many insurers do not recognize extenders as bona fide providers of medical care, they generally do not have established procedures for looking beyond the physician's claim of who provided the service. As a result, many insurers are reimbursing health care providers for services provided by physician extenders.

A field study being conducted by the Social Security Administration may clear up some of the ambiguity surrounding third-party payment. As part of the Social Security Amendments of 1972, Congress authorized the Social Security Administration to conduct a Physician Extender Reimbursement Study. The objective of the study was to "assess the impact on primary care of employing physician extenders and the effects on productivity and Medicare expenditures, of alternative methods of reimbursement" (Gaus et al., 1977: 341). Although the results are yet to be released, they should provide some guidance for insurers in developing reimbursement policies. Legislative attempts have also been made to reduce this barrier to the implementation of the physician extender role. Bills amending the Medicare authorization to allow payment for extender services were introduced into Congress beginning in 1976. Publication of the results of the Social Security study or the passage of amendatory legislation allowing for Medicare payments to physician extenders would reduce barriers to role implementation and increase the likelihood that the training programs could attain their goals.

Program Evaluation and Organizational Effectiveness

It's obvious that the goal-based evaluations of the physician extender training programs had an impact on program performance. The program evaluations defined program success in terms of technical competence. The actions of program administrators were based on this definition. This reduced the variety of information which decision makers took into account in managing program performance. The evaluations embodied a managerial perspective on performance and did not register information pertinent to other constituent perspectives. This interfered with the ability of program administrators to adjust performance to attain the maximum desirable impact. In effect, the evaluations ignored constituent preferences and constraints placed upon the program by the health care delivery system. Because constituent preferences and the nature of system constraints were not explicitly known and acknowledged, program administrators could not very well deal with them in making decisions about organizational action. While the evaluations provided an accurate assessment of the technical performance, they did not generate a realistic assessment of overall program performance. The blind side of these evaluations, in effect, acted as a barrier to the programs' ability to attain desired and desirable ends.

The low variety evaluations had opportunity costs for training programs. The desired impact of program performance could have been substantially increased if information concerning environmental constraints and constituent preferences had been accounted for in the evaluations. There were many strategies open to administrators at relatively low cost which would have aided role implementation in health care practice settings. The programs, for example, could have offered seminars on physician extender practice for practice setting personnel. This would have reduced the ambiguity by providing information and would have eased implementation. Sample job descriptions offered to practice settings might have had the same effect. Given the evaluative definition of effective performance, programs constructed a narrow definition of how they were to perform which did not include such activities. A truly effective training program might have defined its domain as training practice settings in the use of extenders as well as training extenders.

The evaluations of program performance did not provide organizational decision makers with information about the programs' niche and how the niche was changing over time. Armed with information about the nature of environmental factors constraining performance, administrators might have considered pursuing actions which would have reduced barriers to extender practice and the programs' ability to expand the availability of primary health care services. For example, training programs could have actively pursued the placement of extenders in medically underserved areas. They also could have set up liaisons with third-party insurers and state licensing agencies. This might have aided in the development of guidelines sanctioning extender practice and mechanisms for reimbursement of extender services. Such strategies would have heightened the desirable impact of program performance by reducing environmental barriers.

The central point is that the goal-based evaluations examined only a segment of total program performance and did not register other aspects of its impact. This lack of variety affected the ability of decision makers to manage performance so that it had the greatest possible desirable impact on program constituencies and the health care delivery system. As the variety in the case study was increased to better fit the relationship between the training programs and their environment, desirable and undesirable aspects of performance became more readily apparent as did possible actions to heighten the desirable impact of performance. In short, the better the match between the amount and pattern of variety in the evaluative system and organizational performance, the better the quality of information made available to organizational decision makers for managing performance.

Different models of organizational effectiveness would have yielded different interpretations of extender training program performance. The judgments of effectiveness, based on each model's meta criterion, are important since they act as triggering mechanisms for decisions concerning modifications of performance. Decisions are made and actions to modify performance undertaken when it has been judged ineffective. The nature of decisions about and modifications of performance is determined by the meta criterion employed in the evaluation. Comparisons of the judgments flowing from the different models illustrate the importance of meta criteria in determining future organizational action.

The goal-based evaluative model employed in evaluating the extender programs employed a managerial meta criterion, which translated into specific criteria reflecting technical competence. Given the logic of the approach, the programs were judged as performing effectively and no recommendations to modify performance were forthcoming. Since the goal-based approach operates from a predetermined set of goals, the evaluative information "told" decision makers to "do what you've done in the past because it has been successful." There was no questioning the appropriateness of the goals. Constituent preferences and environmental constraints were not accounted for in the evaluative model. The effect was that the evaluations were unlikely to reflect changes in constituent preferences or environmental constraints. The goal-based approach provided a static rendering of organizational performance which assumed that it was taking place within a stable context.

The multiple constituency models present a different array of judgments of training program performance, which vary according to their meta criteria. All the multiple constituency models take a broader view of performance in that they examine constituent perspectives. How these constituent preferences and judgments are interpreted, and the implications for organizational action drawn from the evaluative information, is an altogether different matter. In the case of a multiple constituency evaluation employing a power meta criterion, the performance of the training programs would have been viewed as somewhat ineffective. The most powerful constituency of the extender training programs was physicians within the health care system. They control most of the resources within the system and have the most say in how health care delivery will be organized. It was obvious in the case that the majority of physicians neither trusted extenders nor expected them to be technically competent. Physicians also perceived a possibility that extenders would affect them detrimentally by intruding into areas of health care usually reserved for them. Extenders were, therefore, threatening because they could potentially reduce the demand for physician services. The power meta criterion would have specified that the training programs act in such a way as to mitigate the concerns of physicians. This would probably have resulted in modifications of extender practice which would have reduced their ability to perform the more routine aspects of medical care, thereby reducing the threat to physicians. This, in turn, would have reduced the ability of training programs to increase the supply of primary care services since it was in accomplishing this goal that they came into conflict with the interests of physicians.

The social justice meta criterion, on the other hand, would have paid much more attention to the preferences and concerns of the least advantaged constituency of the training programs, the medically underserved patients whom extenders were supposed to reach. Training program performance would have been judged as somewhat effective since they were expanding the supply of primary health care providers. This, in turn, would have increased the availability of health care services for patients in need of them. Recommendations from this perspective would have run along the lines of increasing the impact of program performance by training more extenders and working toward a better distribution of extenders within the health care system.

The evolutionary meta criterion would yield a judgment of effectiveness similar to that of the social justice approach, but for different reasons. First, the programs were effective in the sense that they were reducing the effect of a constraint on the social system as a whole, the shortage of primary health care providers. But, the programs were also inefficient in that they were not availing themselves of opportunities to heighten the desirable impact of their performance. Recommendations from the evolutionary model would suggest that training programs attempt to heighten the impact of program performance by dealing with constituent concerns and engaging in niche expanding activities, which would relax the constraints imposed on their performance by the health care delivery system.

Although all three multiple constituency models begin their assessments with multiple constituent perspectives, each treats evaluative information in a different manner. Only the evolutionary approach specifies that organizational performance and constituent preferences need to be viewed against the backdrop of the larger system. It is the interplay between constituencies' preferences, actual performance, and context which gives rise to an understanding of organizational effectiveness. The evolutionary meta criterion provides a tool which decision makers can employ in making trade-offs in the satisfactions of preferences. Unlike the power and social justice approaches, the evolutionary meta criterion is not based on the constituent preferences themselves. Rather, it directs attention toward the viability of the larger system, something which is necessary if any constituent preferences are to be fulfilled in the long run. The ultimate judgment of the value of an organization's performance is political in the sense that it is a value-based decision which has to be negotiated by the actors within the system. What the evolutionary approach does is ensure that the variety of constituent perspectives is represented (or at least acknowledged) and that an appreciation of what is possible is gained by the involved parties. Evaluators do not make decisions, they create an informational forum for intelligent decision making.

5

Case Two: Managing Strategic Choice—The Automotive Industry During the 1970s

Evaluating the performance of large organizations is a much more difficult task than the evaluation of smaller organizations. The magnitude of an evaluative effort grows as the size and complexity of an organization increases. Large organizations have more points of contact with and potential impacts on society than their smaller counterparts. They often have more constituencies and constraints defining their niches. The evaluative task becomes more difficult as organizational size and complexity increase.

Very large organizations cannot be evaluated in a formal sense. Formal evaluations of performance would require the creation of large-scale evaluative structures to capture the complexity of overall organizational performance. This is not feasible in most instances. Large-scale evaluative mechanisms would consume large amounts of scarce resources and time. As a result, large organizations must integrate ongoing evaluative mechanisms into their structure which capture the variety in constituent preferences and monitor environmental constraints. This allows an organization to register information about changing preferences and constraints over time. It also creates a *potential* for an organization to respond effectively over time. Organizations with low variety evaluative mechanisms are less likely to register information on changing preferences and constraints, thus reducing the likelihood of adaptive responses to changing conditions.

Registering information on changing preferences and constraints only creates a potential for effective action. In order to realize this potential, organizations must employ decision and planning systems which preserve the variety registered by ongoing evaluation. By preserving variety, organizational decision structures are more likely to take the form of an "argumentative process in the course of which an image of the problem and of the solution emerges gradually among the participants, as a product of incessant judgment, subject to critical argument" (Rittel and Weber, 1973: 162). Information about the changing nature of preferences provides an informational forum in which managers can generate alternative courses of action and select those which appear to have the greatest potential for expanding an organization's niche. It is through niche expanding activities that organizations can satisfy changing constituent preferences and increase the adaptability of the organization/environment over time.

The idea that an organization's structure has an impact on the effectiveness of its performance is not new. The concept has been examined and elaborated on by a number of authors within the structural contingency school of organization theory (e.g., Burns and Stalker, 1962; Lawrence and Lorsch, 1967; Galbraith, 1973).[13] The environment is viewed as a given, something which imposes demands and constraints on the operation of an organization. Demands and constraints are usually characterized as uncertainty generated by the environment, or information processing requirements created by environmental uncertainty. Since the environments of organizations differ, the structural contingency school argues that different organizational structures are required for different environmental circumstances. Hence, the role of management is to understand and design organizations to closely correspond to the demands placed upon them by the environment.

Miles (1980) summarized the thrust of the structural contingency school of thought in terms of the law of requisite variety (see Chapter 3). He noted:

The law of requisite variety and its extensions mean that, in a highly complex environment, a viable organization must possess a corresponding degree of complexity or differentiation in its own structure. In order to cope with uncertainty emanating from the external environment, the organization must create parts that match the attributes of environmental sectors, especially those that pose critical constraints and contingencies for the organization. Thus, this perspective implies that the nature of the external environment *determines*, or at least places constraints on, the choices of organizational designs that will be effective. (Miles, 1980: 250)

13. Structural contingency theory provides a rich conceptual and empirical background for discussions on designing organizations to "fit" different environmental conditions. Interested readers should refer to the original sources. The purpose of this discussion is simply to indicate the convergence of ideas among the structure contingency approach and the social evolutionary model.

In short, organizations must structure themselves to capture environmental variety. By capturing variety in this manner, an organization can create the equivalent of an ongoing evaluative system which registers information about the impact of overall organizational performance. Organizations which do not structurally match the amount and pattern of variety in their environment have a reduced capacity to perceive changes in constituent preferences and environmental constraints. This, in turn, decreases the likelihood that they will perform effectively over time. The following case study examines the changing conditions and preferences encountered by the Big Three automakers during the 1970s and their responses to them. The analysis focuses on the impact of high and low variety organizational structures and control systems on the perception of change and an organization's ability to respond in an environment as it grows increasingly complex.

The Automotive Industry

Fundamental changes are taking place in the structure of the global automotive industry. At the beginning of the 1970s, the automotive industry was composed primarily of national firms serving national markets. By the end of the 1970s, many of the manufacturers were international firms serving the global market. While this transition began long before the 1970s, the decade was a critical period for the U.S. automotive firms and foreshadowed its future evolution.

Over the years, the industry could be viewed as a two-sphere industry: (1) the sales-recordbreaking U.S. manufacturers and (2) foreign manufacturers. Two factors which differentiated the U.S. from other markets were the low price of gasoline and the country's extensive highway system. The U.S., unlike most other industrialized countries, produced enough petroleum at the end of World War II to supply domestic demand. As the U.S. appetite for oil grew to exceed supply during the post war years, federal government price controls kept the price of petroleum products significantly below world levels. This made automotive transportation relatively cheap from the standpoint of the American public. The federal government also funded the construction of the world's most ambitious highway system.

Given these two factors, Americans could indulge their preferences for large, comfortable passenger vehicles. There was no cost penalty associated with owning and operating a large vehicle since gasoline was inexpensive. The road system, built to accommodate large vehicles, encouraged their use. Consequently, the U.S. manufacturers focused on larger passenger vehicles while the rest of the world produced and sold smaller cars. The relative stratification of preferences between U.S. and other customers is reflected in the statistics for U.S. exports and imports. From 1960 to 1969, U.S. automakers shipped an annual average of 3.3 percent of their production to markets outside of the U.S. (Motor Vehicle Manufacturers Association [MVMA], 1980: 21). During the same period, approximately 8.8 percent of the passenger vehicles sold annually in the U.S. were imports (see Table 5-2). These were standard-size vehicles by world standards but relatively small by American standards.

The relative size of the U.S. automotive market also set it apart from other national markets. In 1940, Americans owned 73.9 percent of the world's passenger vehicles and 55.7 percent of the trucks and buses. By 1978, ownership outside the U.S. had increased substantially and American ownership had declined to 39.2 percent of the world's passenger vehicles and 39.0 percent of trucks and buses (MVMA, 1980: 27).[14] The world-wide increase in vehicle ownership reflected a number of factors, particularly the globally rising standard of living. As automotive products became more affordable to persons in other nations, world automotive production increased to meet growing demand. In 1940, for example, 4.9 million automotive vehicles were produced. By 1978, global production had increased to 42.4 million units (MVMA, 1980: 14).

The U.S. automotive companies led the movement to satisfy growing global demand. Ford began manufacturing vehicles outside of North America and GM began exporting vehicles prior to World War I. General Motors followed Ford's lead in the 1920s by acquiring manufacturing capabilities outside the U.S. By 1973, GM, Ford, and Chrysler were each manufacturing over one million vehicles outside of North America. Of the three firms, Ford was the most internationally oriented. In 1973, 30 percent of its vehicles were manufactured outside the U.S. compared to 18 percent for GM (Bloomfield, 1978). Even as the U.S. firms were expanding their global operations, several new companies were formed to serve growing demand in the new national markets, particularly in Western Europe and Japan.

As global competition increased, the leadership of the U.S. manufacturers decreased. Although U.S. manufacturers have had overseas production and assembly facilities for many years, a marked movement toward even more international production began during the 1960s. One

14. The U.S. has 6 percent of the world's population and remains the world's largest single national market.

reason for this development was the greater sales opportunities abroad. Also, the sales growth rate in the U.S. was slowing as population growth slowed. A greater potential for new growth existed in the developing countries. Table 5-1 shows automobile ownership by population in various regions. The North American market (U.S. and Canada) was the most "saturated," with one motor vehicle for every one and a half persons in 1978. Similarly, the ratio of persons to vehicles was relatively low in Western Europe, Japan, and Oceania (Australia, New Zealand, and surrounding areas). The areas with the greatest potential for growth were Asia, Africa, Eastern Europe, Central America, and South America. The export strategy that many automotive firms had pursued to compete in the developed countries markets was not suitable for entry into these new markets since many developing nations placed local content restrictions on auto imports. These restrictions required that anywhere from 50 to 95 percent of the components of vehicles sold in the country be locally fabricated ("To A Global Car," 1978). Consequently, participation in the regions of the world that had the greatest potential for growth increasingly required operations abroad.

Table 5-1. Ratio of Population to Motor Vehicles by World Regions

Region	Population/ Passenger Vehicles	Population/ Total Vehicles
North America	1.9	1.5
Oceania	3.1	2.5
Western Europe	3.6	3.3
Japan	5.4	3.4
South America	18.0	14.0
Eastern Europe	24.0	16.0
Central America	22.0	16.0
Africa	79.0	54.0
Asia	338.0	188.0

SOURCE: Motor Vehicle Manufacturers Association, *World Motor Vehicle Data,* Detroit: Motor Vehicles Manufacturers Association of the U.S., Inc., 1980, pp. 25-27.

Another factor accelerating the emergence of an international automotive market was the narrowing of the gap between world and U.S. energy prices. As energy prices in the U.S. moved upward toward world levels, American preferences began to shift to more fuel efficient vehicles. The preferences of West Europeans also shifted as their higher standard of living permitted more comfortably appointed vehicles. The effect was a convergence of preferences. The distinct product characteristics associated with vehicles produced in the U.S., as opposed to elsewhere, began to blur ("Detroit's Uphill Battle," 1980; "Industry Changes Tied to Worldwide Character," 1977). Changes in U.S. imports and exports during the late 1970s reflected this. The annual import share of sales increased to an average 18.3 percent during 1975-9, up from 8.8 percent during the 1960s (see Table 5-2). This occurred even as the U.S. automakers downsized their vehicles to increase fuel efficiency. The downsizing and redesign of American-produced vehicles, however, made them more competitive in international markets. For the same period, annual exports rose to an average 8.2 percent of the U.S. manufacturers' production, up from 3.3 percent during the 1960s (MVMA, 1980: 21).

The convergence of consumer preferences world-wide had two important effects on the industry. First, it made the industry more competitive on an international level by reducing trade barriers. Second, it ushered in the concept of world vehicle design. The world vehicle concept is based on the idea that a single design can be appropriate for all national markets. GM describes world vehicles as "cars and trucks which are produced in several different countries, yet share the same basic design and as many common or interchangeable parts as possible while still accommodating the demands of local customers and government requirements. A key factor behind a world vehicle is to have components produced in plants serving several countries so that volume production will minimize costs" (General Motors Corporation, 1980: 65). The world vehicle did not become a practical idea until the differences between the U.S. and other markets were minimized by rising gasoline prices. Producers then gave greater emphasis to designing vehicles suited for the international market as opposed to the earlier practice of designing many vehicles to service different national markets.

The movement toward internationalization of the industry was accelerated by rapidly increasing gasoline prices in 1979-80 and the ensuing global recession, which threw the automotive industry into turmoil. Sales of U.S. and West European manufacturers declined as the fuel economy of Japanese vehicles became more attractive to consumers world-wide. U.S. manufacturers had begun downsizing during the mid-1970s; but consumer preferences for fuel economy outpaced the firms' timetable for bringing their most fuel efficient designs into production. The European manufacturers suffered from a similar problem. They were producing more mid-size vehicles than their consumers were willing to purchase. The result was that the Japanese manufacturers increased their sales significantly at the expense of U.S. and European firms. They were, in effect, producing the right car at the right time.

One indicator of the gains posted by the Japanese automakers was the relative rates of increase in production from the late 1960s to the late 1970s for American, West European, and Japanese producers (MVMA, 1980: 14). The average annual production for the automotive companies in each of these regions from 1965-9 was: U.S.—10.28 million units, Western Europe (Great Britain, Germany, France, and Italy)—8.88 million units, and Japan—2.7 million units. From 1975-9, average annual production was: U.S.—11.46 million units, Western Europe—10.34 million units, Japan—8.4 million units. The increases in production between these two periods were 11.5 percent, 16.4 percent, and 311.1 percent, respectively. During the first six months of 1980, Japan became the number one automotive manufacturing nation by outproducing the U.S. manufacturers 5.46 million to 4.42 million units ("Inside Japan: The New No. 1," 1980). It was the first time in automotive history that the automotive firms of any nation had outproduced the U.S. manufacturers.

The long-term effect of increased competition and the changes in the international structure of the industry is likely to be a substantial consolidation of automotive manufacturers during the next decade. Auto industry analyst, Arvid Jouppi, suggested that the industry will consist of firms able to produce at least 2 million units per year and able to penetrate most regional markets ("The Auto Clash Goes Global," 1978). Donald Petersen, president of Ford Motor Company, was more specific. He foresaw only eight companies in that league.[15] He noted, "I'm certainly not suggesting that Rolls-Royce, Mercedes-Benz, and other low volume producers should start to worry. But it is obvious that many smaller specialized companies are going to survive only in marginal or protected markets. Few of them can afford the astronomical cost of developing new models without associating with larger companies or turning directly to government for loans, subsidies, or even partnerships" ("Detroit: Hitting the Skids," 1980: 59).

Consolidation within the industry will increase in the future. Some consolidation will occur through outright acquisition of existing automotive companies, such as Peugeot's acquisition of Citroen in 1975 and the Chrysler-Europe companies in 1978. Some will occur through equity participation, such as Renault's equity position in AMC. Joint ventures

---

15. Only five companies had production exceeding 2 million units in 1979—GM, Ford, Toyota, Nissan, and Volkswagen (MVMA, 1980: 11).

to avoid trade barriers and service local markets will become more common. BL (formerly British Leyland) and Honda Motor Company, for example, planned to jointly produce mid-size vehicles in Britain for sale in the Common Market countries. Alfa-Romeo and Nissan Motor Company reportedly will jointly produce 60,000 small vehicles yearly by 1983 for sale in Italy. Other joint ventures will be undertaken to reduce manufacturing costs through joint production and the use of common components. Saab-Scania and Lancia, for example, set up a joint venture in 1979 to build mid-size sedans by 1985. The vehicles will be customized to suit each producer and will use a number of common components.

In summary, changes in the international automotive industry occurred rapidly during the 1970s as the price of gasoline increased and consumer preferences converged. What had once been an industry of national firms serving national markets was becoming one of international firms serving a global market. Competition within the industry was vigorous and unrelenting and it was likely that only a handful of today's firms would emerge as independent global manufacturers in the 1990s. Within this context, U.S. automotive manufacturers had to cope with significant changes in their domestic market as well as within those occurring internationally.

The U.S. Automotive Market

The economic climate in which the U.S. automotive manufacturers operated from 1946-72 can be characterized as one of long-term stability with short-term insecurity. It was stable in that motor vehicle sales steadily increased from 4.0 million units in 1947 to 13.0 million units in 1972 (Ward's 1948; 1974). There were no significant shifts in consumer preferences for automotive products during this period. Most everything the automakers offered was well received with few exceptions, such as the Edsel. Industry executives and managers retained a large degree of discretion since the automotive marketplace was virtually free from government regulation. The price and supply of gasoline remained stable with adequate supplies available to the consuming public.

Short-term insecurity was caused by the competitive nature of the market. Competition among manufacturers was based on product differentiation, with the goal of each manufacturer being a larger yearly share of sales. Each firm was constantly trying to outdo its competitors by developing products that would capture the public's imagination. Substantial financial rewards were attached to success. Since the lead times for the development and production of a new vehicle ran from three to five years, a company that beat its competitors to the market with a new product that the public liked would enjoy sales success and profitability. The Ford Mustang was a good example of this. Introduced in 1964, the Mustang pioneered a new product segment in the automotive market. GM did not have a comparable vehicle in production. The result was that Ford had the compact specialty segment virtually to itself until GM introduced the Camaro in 1967.

Short-term predictability is a necessary ingredient for production planning. Each firm has to predict what its sales by model would be in the short run so that parts can be ordered and plants equipped to build them. Inaccurate predictions result in either a shortage of vehicles and a loss of sales or inventory buildups with associated costs. Both situations adversely affect corporate profitability. If a competitor produces a vehicle which is better received by the public, the firm's production scheduling is thrown into disarray as adjustments are made to fit the shifting sales picture. Loss of sales means that inventories accumulate, expensive plant and equipment are idled, and the firm's profits suffer. Hence, the intense competition among automotive companies creates a sense of short-term insecurity within a market which, heretofore, could have been characterized as having considerable long-term stability.

The relative success of the Big Three manufacturers (GM, Ford, and Chrysler) during the 1946-72 period was reflected in the share of sales each held. The year-to-year variations, shown in Table 5-2, provide an indication of the shifting fortunes of each automaker in the competitive market. During this period, GM's sales share peaked at 51.8 percent in 1962, declining to 44.4 percent in 1972. Ford's share peaked in 1954 when it held a 30.8 percent sales share, a position which gradually declined to 24.3 percent in 1972. Chrysler's high of 25.7 percent in 1946 eroded steadily to a low of 9.6 percent in 1962. The company recouped part of its losses through the 1960s to a 13.8 percent share in 1972.

Overall erosion in the U.S. sales shares of the domestic automotive manufacturers from the mid-1960s through the early 1970s occurred because of increased import penetration of the domestic market. The import share of sales increased from 6.1 percent in 1965 to 15.1 percent in 1973. Gottesman (1975) pointed out that most of the growth in the domestic market during this period went to the imports.

One accepted practice to determine a market's growth is to measure the increase from one peak year to the next. In 1965, 8,763 million domestically made cars were sold in the U.S. The next peak year was 1973 when 9,676 million units were purchased. In those nine years, 1965 to '73 sales of U.S.-made cars grew only at a 1.1% annual rate. However, the overall domestic market grew a total of 2.12 million units. Imports, meanwhile, took off from 559,430 units in '65 to 2,437,345 in 1973. So, comparing these peak years imports grabbed 88% of total U.S. market growth. (Gottesman, 1975: 19)

Table 5-2: Market Shares by Corporation: 1946-1979

Year	GM	Ford	Chrysler	Other Domestic[1]	Imports
1946	37.7	21.9	25.7	14.5	—
1947	41.8	21.0	21.7	15.2	—
1948	40.6	18.8	21.4	18.6	0.4
1949	42.8	21.3	21.4	14.2	0.2
1950	45.4	24.0	17.6	12.8	0.2
1951	42.8	22.1	21.8	12.8	0.4
1952	41.7	22.7	21.2	13.4	0.7
1953	45.0	25.1	20.3	9.0	0.5
1954	50.7	30.8	12.9	5.0	0.5
1955	50.7	27.6	16.8	4.0	0.8
1956	50.7	28.4	15.4	3.6	1.6
1957	44.8	30.3	18.3	3.0	3.4
1958	46.3	26.4	13.9	5.2	8.1
1959	42.1	28.1	11.3	8.3	10.1
1960	43.6	26.6	14.0	8.2	7.5
1961	46.5	28.5	10.7	7.7	6.4
1962	51.8	26.3	9.6	7.3	4.8
1963	51.0	24.8	12.3	6.6	5.1
1964	49.0	26.0	13.8	5.1	6.0
1965	50.0	25.4	14.6	3.7	6.1
1966	48.1	26.0	15.3	3.1	7.3
1967	49.5	22.1	16.0	3.0	9.3
1968	46.7	23.7	16.2	2.9	10.4
1969	46.7	24.2	15.1	2.6	11.2
1970	39.7	26.4	16.0	3.1	14.6
1971	45.1	23.5	13.7	2.6	15.0
1972	44.4	24.3	13.8	3.0	14.5
1973	44.3	23.5	13.3	3.5	15.1
1974	41.8	24.9	13.5	3.9	15.7
1975	43.3	23.0	11.7	3.8	18.1
1976	47.2	22.4	12.9	2.6	14.8
1977	46.3	22.6	10.9	1.7	18.2
1978	47.6	22.9	10.1	1.5	17.7
1979	46.4	20.3	9.0	1.6	22.6

SOURCE: *Automotive News*, April 30, 1980, p. 15. Reprinted, with adaptations, by permission of the publisher.

[1] Includes AMC and predecessors, Studebaker-Packard, Kaiser-Frazer, Willys, and Misc. Domestic.

Increased competition in the domestic maket was a harbinger of things to come as the changes in the international market accelerated.

The domestic market stability of the 1950s and 1960s quickly gave way to turbulence during the 1970s. The 1973-79 period began with a mixed year for the automakers. While an all-time record 11.35 million passenger vehicles were sold during 1973, it also marked the beginning of the end of the era of cheap energy in the United States as the Organization of Petroleum Exporting Countries placed an oil embargo on the U.S. Passenger vehicle sales plummeted to 8.7 million units in 1974, as energy supplies tightened during the first quarter and the economy slipped into a recession during the later half of the year. The recession dampened sales through 1975, when only 8.26 million units were sold. Volume picked up in 1976 and continued to gain through 1978, as growing demand pushed the sales of figures over the 10 million unit mark in each of those years. Sales contracted again in 1979-80 in the face of rapidly increasing gasoline prices and world-wide recession.

Variations in total volume tell only part of the story. Consumer preferences, which had been relatively stable, seesawed back and forth between large and small vehicles. During the 1973-4 embargo, consumers began buying smaller, more fuel efficient vehicles and shunning the larger cars that had been the mainstay of domestic production. Inventories of full-size vehicles quickly accumulated and the manufacturers shifted their production emphasis to the smallest vehicles in their product lines. As the economy pulled out of the recession and the price of gasoline stabilized, consumer preferences shifted back to larger vehicles. By 1976, the manufacturers had a glut of small cars and could not produce enough large vehicles to satisfy demand. This pattern of consumption continued until 1979 when gasoline prices began increasing very rapidly. Huge inventories of large vehicles built up as sales declined. The domestic manufacturers shifted production back to smaller vehicles, but the consumers demanded better fuel economy than they were able to offer. The result was that Japanese imports increased their share of the domestic market significantly, to 22.6 percent in 1979, at the domestic automakers' expense.

The impact of the 1979-80 sales downturn was disastrous. By mid-1980, almost a quarter of a million employees of the Big Three were on indefinite layoff, domestic vehicle sales were at their lowest point in almost twenty years, and the monthly import share of sales had passed the 40 percent mark in April. Losses for the industry at year end totaled over $4 billion. General Motors posted a $763 million loss, its first in fifty-nine years. Ford Motor Company lost $1.5 billion, the largest loss in its history. Chrysler Corporation recorded a loss for the third consecutive year and was being kept afloat by federal loan guarantees. Chrysler's 1.7 billion dollar loss was the largest ever reported by a U.S. industrial corporation. These losses came at a time when the industry was being forced to undertake a massive capital investment program to design and produce small, fuel efficient vehicles that would be competitive on the emerging international automotive scene. GM alone planned to spend $40 billion between 1980-5, with the industry total approaching $75 billion ("Losing a Big Segment . . . ," 1980). While the prognosis for the industry had been bright as it moved into the 1970s, predictions for the 1980s were not as optimistic.

The factors which led to this state of affairs in the domestic market were intimately tied to the changes occurring in the international automotive industry environment. The following section reviews changes in three major environmental constraints which occurred during the 1970s. Two of them, energy and import competition, reflected changes in the international environment. The other, government regulation, was peculiar to the domestic market but interacted with the others to affect the industry's ability to modify its performance to fit its evolving niche. The way in which the Big Three perceived and responded to changes in these factors was reflected in their relative sales positions as they entered the 1980s.

Energy, Government Regulation, and the Imports

Price and Supply of Gasoline

Historically, U.S. automakers paid little attention to the price and supply of gasoline. Its availability was taken for granted, something which existed in cheap and plentiful supply. Domestic oil production supplied most of the American consumers' needs through the early post war years. The low price of gasoline gave the automakers considerable freedom in product design. There was little concern about fuel efficiency.

The domestic appetite for energy grew considerably after World War II, and the economy became increasingly dependent on foreign supplies of crude oil. Domestic prices were kept substantially below world levels through government controls. The situation changed significantly with the 1973-4 oil embargo, which took basic pricing decisions out of the hands of the American oil companies and the federal government. The embargo marked the beginning of a series of gasoline price hikes and heightened consumer uncertainty about the continued availability of petroleum products.

In 1973, the average price of a gallon of regular leaded gasoline was $.39. Prices increased by a third to slightly over $.52 per gallon at the end of the embargo in March, 1974. As can be seen in Table 5-3, price increases slowed through 1975-8 but moved rapidly upward in 1979. By October, 1979, the average price of gasoline passed the $1.00 per gallon mark, with the January to December increase totaling almost 50 percent. Prices continued to increase through 1980, with year end prices almost 40 percent above those at the end of the previous year.

Table 5-3: Average Retail Prices for Gasoline: 1973-1980

Years	Leaded Regular	Unleaded Regular	Leaded Premium	Average for All Grades
	(cents per gallon, including tax)			
1973	39.0	NA	NA	NA
1974	53.2	NA	56.9	NA
1975	56.7	NA	60.9	NA
1976	59.0	61.4	63.6	NA
1977	62.2	65.6	67.4	NA
1978	62.6	67.0	69.4	65.2
1979	85.7	90.3	92.2	88.2
1980[1]	119.0	124.4	127.8	122.0

[1] January to November, 1980 average.
SOURCE: U.S. Energy Information Administration, *Monthly Energy Review*, (January, 1981), p. 81; and (July, 1976), p. 54.

Both automotive sales and travel were sensitive to changes in the price and perceived supply of gasoline. Sales of automotive vehicles quickly turned downward when prices were rapidly increasing and uncertainty existed about its availability. The automakers had never really considered the sensitivity of automotive sales to the price and supply of gasoline as important parameters of their operations prior to the early 1970s. Changes in the price and perceived supply of gasoline were the underlying factors which created the marked volatility they faced during the 1970s. Expensive gasoline also made the imports' relative fuel economy more attractive to the consumer, and government safety and emissions control mandates more difficult to meet.

Government Regulation

The second factor which changed significantly from the mid-1960s through the late 1970s was government regulation of the automotive industry. In 1965, automotive products were virtually unregulated. By 1979, many aspects of product design had become heavily regulated. The auto industry encountered three successive regulatory initiatives in the areas of automotive safety, emissions control, and fuel economy. The regulations changed the nature of the products the firms could offer and redefined the limits of managerial discretion in a number of areas.

Safety. In 1966, Congress passed the National Traffic and Motor Vehicle Safety Act, which was the first major federal initiative in regulating automotive vehicles. Passage of the Highway Safety Act of 1970 created the National Highway Traffic Safety Administration (NHTSA) and charged it with enforcement of all automotive safety regulations. By the end of 1973, forty-four federal safety standards applied to one or more classifications of motor vehicles. The Motor Vehicle Manufacturers Association estimated that buyers of new model cars were paying a collective $3.3 billion safety premium annually (Ward's, 1974). By 1980, the number of regulations governing automotive safety had more than doubled from their 1973 level. Safety standards covered many aspects of automotive design. Standards were issued which mandated passenger restraint systems, integrity of various components, the structural strength of the automotive body, and so on. The safety laws also authorized NHTSA to initiate recalls for product defects, which became an increasingly expensive part of safety regulation during the 1970s. Between 1974 and 1976, recalls averaged less than three million vehicles per year. Recalls increased significantly during the late 1970s, adding to the industry's operating expenses and reducing the automakers' credibility. In 1977, for example, 12.6 million vehicles were recalled (Ward's, 1978).

These safety regulations changed the niche in which the automotive companies operated, by reducing managerial discretion over the design of automotive products. This constrained the ability of managers to operate as they had in the past.

Emissions Control. In 1966, Congress passed the Motor Vehicle Air Pollution Act, which charged the Department of Health, Education, and Welfare with setting emissions standards for new motor vehicles. The standards, issued in 1966, required that 1968 model vehicles emit no more than 6.3 grams per mile (gm/mi) hydrocarbons and 51 gm/mi carbon monoxide. This represented 42 percent and 56 percent reductions in hydrocarbon and carbon monoxide emissions from the uncontrolled levels of 1960. The Air Quality Act of 1967 further increased the federal role in emissions control. The law gave the federal government the sole responsibility for setting emissions standards for new vehicles and further reduced the allowable levels of hydrocarbon and carbon monoxide emissions.

As public concern about environmental quality continued to increase, Congress passed the Clean Air Act of 1970. Its purpose was to set future standards and enforcement procedures for stationary and nonstationary sources of air pollutants. The newly formed Environmental Protection Agency (EPA) was charged with enforcement of the act and issued standards in April, 1971. The new standards for 1975 called for emissions levels of no more than .41 gm/mi hydrocarbons, 3.4 gm/mi carbon monoxide, and .4 gm/mi nitrous oxides. These levels were 90 percent reductions from the 1970 emissions levels set by earlier air pollution laws.

While Table 5-4 shows an orderly progression over time for the reduction of emissions, the actual schedule was continually changing. The automakers hoped that the tough standards set in 1970 would be

Table 5-4: Federal Emissions Control Standards: 1968-1985

| Year | Grams Per Mile | | |
	Hydrocarbons	Carbon Monoxide	Nitrous Oxide
Prior to Control (1960)	15.0	90.0	5.0
1968	6.3	51.0	5.0
1970	4.1	34.0	5.0
1972	3.0	28.0	5.0
1973	3.0	28.0	3.1
(1975 as specified in CAA of 1970)	(.41)	(3.4)	(.4)
1975	1.5	15.0	3.1
1976	1.5	15.0	3.1
1977	1.5	15.0	2.0
1978	1.5	15.0	2.0
1979	1.5	15.0	2.0
1980	.41	7.0	2.0
1981	.41	3.4	1.0
1982	.41	3.4	1.0
1983	.41	3.4	1.0
1984	.41	3.4	1.0
1985	.41	3.4	1.0

SOURCE: Compiled from various sources by the author.

relaxed or delayed, but actions doing so in 1973 and 1977 did not occur until immediately before the standards for each year were to go into effect. This created an extremely uncertain situation for the automakers since they did not know what standards they would have to meet for models in and often nearing the end of the product design process.

Fuel Economy. The third regulatory initiative concerned fuel economy, which became an issue because of the 1973-4 Arab oil embargo. The embargo caught the federal government by surprise. It had nothing which could be considered an energy policy, the result of neglect based on earlier U.S. energy independence. It became obvious in the wake of the embargo that the government had to move quickly toward a comprehensive energy strategy. The first reaction to the embargo came from President Ford in the form of voluntary restrictions on Sunday driving, voluntary reductions in gas station hours of operation, a national 55 mile per hour speed limit, and other stopgap measures. The Ford Administration realized that any long-term strategy would have to take into consideration the effects of automotive vehicles on energy consumption. In 1973, transportation used 25 percent of all primary energy supplied in the U.S. Most of this usage was in the form of petroleum products and represented 53 percent of nation's petroleum usage in the United States (General Motors Corporation, 1974). Hence, it was evident that reducing the fuel consumption of automotive vehicles would play an important role in any long-term energy policy.

In an October, 1974, televised address, President Ford called on the Big Three automakers to voluntarily increase the fuel economy of their new car fleets to 18.7 miles per gallon (mpg) by the 1980 model year. The fleet mileage averages for the 1974 model year were: GM—12.2, Ford—14.4, and Chrysler—13.8 miles per gallon. The 1980 target required 53, 30, and 36 percent improvements in each of the manufacturer's fleets (General Motors Corporation, 1975). The automakers' position was that they could meet the voluntary target if emissions levels remained the same through 1980 and moratoriums were declared on significant new safety regulations in the near term. With these caveats, the automakers publicly committed themselves to meeting the fuel economy target.

Congress then enacted the Energy Policy and Conservation Act of 1975, which translated the voluntary agreement into law over the mixed opposition of the automakers. The voluntary agreement had set an 18.7 mpg target for 1980, which the automakers felt was technologically feasible. The act reset the 1980 target at 20 mpg and added a more stringent 27.5 standard for the 1985 model year. Table 5-5 shows the year to year progression of the fuel economy standards.

Table 5-5: Federal Fuel Economy Standards: 1977-1985

Model Year	Miles Per Gallon[1]
1978	18.0
1979	19.0
1980	20.0
1981	22.0
1982	24.0
1983	26.0
1984	27.0
1985	27.5

[1] Fleet Sales weighted average
SOURCE: Compiled from various sources by the author.

Import Competition

The third major factor was import competition. From 1946-55, imports collectively held less than 1 percent of the domestic market (see Table 5-2). Imports rapidly increased their share of sales to 10.1 percent in 1959, as domestic vehicles became more outlandishly styled, larger, and more expensive. The Big Three introduced their first compacts in 1959—the GM Corvair, the Ford Falcon, and the Chrysler Valiant—to slow down the imports' market penetration. These domestic compacts were larger and more expensive than the imports, but smaller and less expensive than the standard domestic autos. Their market performance was better than the automakers expected. Import sales slipped for three consecutive years, dropping below a 5 percent market share in 1962. But, through the 1960s, the domestic compacts gained in size and price and their sales began to decline. The imports regained their lost market share and, by 1968, again held over 10 percent of the market.

The U.S. producers attempted to halt this trend again by introducing new lines of small cars. Ford introduced the Maverick in 1969, which was based on a shortened version of two Ford compacts, the Ford Falcon and the Mustang. In 1970, both Ford and GM introduced small cars, the Pinto and the Vega. Although these were the smallest cars Ford and GM manufactured, they did not compete directly with the imports in either size or price. The Maverick, for example, was almost two feet longer, 700 pounds heavier, and a couple of hundred dollars more expensive than the best selling import, the VW Beetle.

Two factors explain the reluctance of the automakers to compete directly with the imports through domestic production. The first was related to the image the automakers had of imports and import buyers. Rukeyser (1969: 112-3) summed up the Big Three executives' outlook toward them in the following:

Self interest and sentiment are no less closely intertwined among auto executives than among other mortals. These executives have a visceral aversion to small, austere cars that cannot be wholly accounted for by their reading of the economics of their business. By all evidence, these men truly love the products of their factories. They have grown used to accepting each year that their cars are the best and most beautiful ever, as well as the biggest, until these three terms have become almost synonymous in their own thinking as in the prose of their ad writers. It is hard for them—as for the majority of their fellow Americans—to see any but negative virtues in the small imported car. Consequently, it is hard for them to imagine that any sane, patriotic, and unimpoverished citizen could find such a car desirable. When forced to think about the sales statistics of foreign cars, auto executives almost invariably begin their analysis by pointing to the mindless lust of all things foreign that supposedly holds great segments of the consuming public in thrall. From there it is but a short hop to the conclusion that there is no point in Detroit's trying to match the imports in price and specifications, since even if, by heroic effort, Detroit could do this, the perverse buyer would still shun the domestic product.

Big Three executives couldn't understand why anyone would want a small, uncomfortable car when large, luxurious domestic models were readily available. According to industry executives, it could only be snobbery. Henry Ford II, for example, remarked that "there's a distinct snob appeal to owning one of those cars," referring to the VW Beetle ("Ford and the Future," 1971: 29). John Riccardo drew a similar conclusion soon after ascending to the presidency of Chrysler. He noted that "part of the psychology of the foreign cars' success is snob appeal" ("Chrysler: A Whole New Ball Game," 1970: 25).

The second factor was profit. Small cars were, simply, less profitable than larger cars. Production costs of large and small vehicles are comparable. Assembly requires a large amount of hand labor regardless of vehicle size. Material costs between large and small vehicles are not strikingly different. Most of the small-car savings are in steel and iron, two relatively inexpensive materials. Also, much of the profit from auto sales is generated by the options a customer purchases. The margins on options are significantly higher than that on the base price of the vehicle. Small-car buyers tend to buy fewer options than large-car purchasers, which also reduced the profitability of small vehicles.

Rukeyser (1969: 112) explained the cost structure clearly in terms of the prices of 1970 model year vehicles. He noted:

As the size and selling price of a car are reduced, then the profit margin tends to drop even faster. A standard U.S. sedan with a basic price of $3,000, for example, yields something like $250 to $300 profit to its manufacturer. But when the price falls by a third, to $2,000, the factory profit drops by about half. Below $2,000, the decline grows ever more precipitous. And the bad news does not stop there. "Not only is the profit margin per car smaller," says J. Wilner Sundelson, an independent economist with long experience in the industry, "but the chance that the customer will buy a lot of optional equipment is less. What's attracting the customer in the first place is the low price and low cost of operation. Something with a $2,000 price tag isn't going to have $700 worth of options added to it, whereas a car with a $3,000 price tag could."

The automakers were, therefore, willing to concede the lower end of the automotive market to the import competition since it was the least profitable market segment. As the industry entered the 1970s, the automakers were attempting to keep the import market share from getting any larger, through the introduction of their own small vehicles. As Table 5-2 shows, they were not very sucessful. By 1979, the import share of sales in the U.S. market climbed to 22.6 percent.

Summary

The cumulative impact of changes in these three factors dramatically altered the domestic niche in which the Big Three operated. Government intervention through safety and emissions standards began increasing the volatility of the automakers' environment by reducing managerial discretion over vehicle design. While reducing managerial discretion, the safety and emissions control regulations were not earthshaking in themselves. From 1967 to 1974, the manufacturers dealt with these new constraints by adding weight to existing vehicle designs. Structural strength, for example, was increased by adding more structural steel to the frame and body of a vehicle. Automotive emissions were reduced to meet emissions standards by detuning engines. Reductions in engine performance and the added weight to meet safety regulations were compensated for by installing larger engines. These strategies for meeting government regulations required minimal product innovation. Rather, they represented tinkering with existing automotive designs. The sum effect of the strategies was the reduction of the average fuel economy of vehicles offered to the public from 1967 to 1974.

Adding weight to vehicle designs carried few penalties in the marketplace as long as gasoline was cheap and plentiful. The increased weight added relatively little to the cost of operating an automotive vehicle. The situation changed radically under conditions of high prices and scarcity. With the inception of federal fuel economy standards, government regulation began to impose opposing demands on the automakers. The fuel economy standards required that the manufacturers increase average mileage per gallon, which could be accomplished only by reducing vehicle weight. What the government was demanding by the mid-1970s was that the automakers build safe, low emissions, high mileage automotive vehicles, something which the industry viewed as being a contradiction of terms. The sum effect of all three sets of regulations was that the automakers were being required to re-think and re-engineer automotive transportation in a relatively short period of time. While automotive engineering had been a stagnant field during the 1950s and 1960s, the 1970s challenged automotive engineers as they had not been challenged before.

Volatility of demand and strong import competition aggravated the situation. The significant redesign efforts mandated by government regulation required massive investments in product research and development, product design and engineering, retooling, and new plants. Imports impeded the Big Three's efforts by capturing continually larger shares of a shrinking market. While it had been possible to ignore import competition as long as the market was growing and the automakers were posting yearly production and sales increases, rising import market penetration posed a real threat to the Big Three as the size of the U.S. market declined. By reducing the share and volume of the U.S. automakers, the imports were effectively reducing the automakers' ability to fund their capital investment and product design programs.

In short, a historically stable environment was becoming increasingly turbulent as the constraints which defined the automakers' niche changed. Massive product innovations were required to meet the demands of the government and the consumer. Financing these efforts was being hampered by the increased market penetration of imports in a shrinking market. Survival hinged on the automakers' ability to rapidly change to fit into their evolving domestic and international niche.

The Automakers' Responses to Strategic Change

The responses of the automakers to these changes varied from firm to firm. The following will focus on General Motors and compare actions of Ford and Chrysler to its actions. Being the largest firm in the industry, GM had the largest stake in the changing environment. GM had the most employees, the largest bodies of dealers, shareholders, and customers. In many ways, GM was also the least prepared of the automakers to meet the challenges of the 1970s. It had been the most profitable auto-maker because its operations focused on the most profitable part of the market, the full-sized/luxury segment. As a result, GM had the lowest average fleet fuel economy of the Big Three in the early 1970s. The fuel economy standards enacted in 1975 required that GM improve its vehi-cle fuel economy performance by 125 percent by 1985, 25 percent more than either Ford or Chrysler. GM also had the greatest investment in plant and equipment designed to produce large automobiles.

General Motors management was criticized on a number of fronts during the late 1960s and early 1970s. John DeLorean, a rising star in the GM management hierarchy during those years who left the firm in the early 1970s, characterized General Motors management as being out of touch with reality. He claimed that the short-term, financial orientation of top management was undermining the future of the firm (Wright, 1979). General Motors was also under fire because it was the largest industrial corporation in the U.S. The federal government sporadically discussed the possibility of initiating antitrust actions against the firm. Consumer groups complained about the quality of GM products. Envi-ronmentalists waged campaigns against the corporation over pollution created by the vehicles it produced. Workers in many of GM's plants were extremely dissatisfied with their jobs, as characterized by the Lordstown assembly plant strike and the similar problems at its Tarry-town, New Jersey, assembly facility in the early 1970s.

In 1970, General Motors entered into a confrontation with Ralph Nader. Nader organized the Project on Corporate Responsibility, which was attempting to reform corporate governance through the shareholder proxy process. The project selected GM as its target and purchased a few shares of GM stock, allowing it to submit shareholder resolutions for the 1970 annual meeting. The dynamics of the process which sur-rounded this effort, commonly known as Campaign GM, and the actions which followed it are illustrative of the transformation which GM under-went during the early 1970s.

Campaign GM submitted nine resolutions to the corporation for inclusion on the 1970 proxy statement. Only two survived GM's opposi-tion before the Securities and Exchange Commission. One called for the establishment of a shareholder committee on corporate responsibility, the other the addition of three public directors to the GM board. GM conducted an extensive lobbying effort to defeat the resolutions. It enclosed a twenty-two page booklet entitled "GM's Record of Pro-gress" with the proxy statement mailed to the shareholders. It also took out full page advertisements in 150 newspapers, which described GM's efforts in the areas of automotive safety, pollution control, mass transit, plant safety, and social welfare. Although both proposals were unsuccessful, they had an impact. Management was concerned because a number of institutional investors voted in favor of the resolutions or for management's position while submitting letters expressing concern over the issues.[16] In the months following the 1970 annual meeting, GM undertook a number of actions, which if not initiated by the institutional investor response to Campaign GM, were spurred on by it.

General Motors, for example, established a board-level Public Policy Committee composed of five outside directors. The committee was charged with the responsibility of exploring all phases of GM's products and operations that related to matters of public policy. The committee met and listened to the views of corporate outsiders, many of them critical of GM's role in American society. In one of its first recommendations, the committee suggested that GM form a scientific advisory panel to advise the board on technological and scientific matters, particularly in the area of the effect of GM's products and operations on the environment. The resulting panel was composed of six distinguished scientists and headed by Nobel Laureate Charles H. Townes. The firm also upgraded its pollution control efforts by creating a vice presidency for environmental activities. A noted authority on air pollution, Ernest Starkman from the University of California, was appointed to fill the position. An effort to broaden the perspective of the board resulted in the appointment of Dr. Leon Sullivan, a prominent black civil rights leader. The firm also convened a conference for a group of educators, political figures, and institutional investors to explain GM's efforts in a variety of areas of public concern. This effort was later transformed into the *General Motors' Public Interest Report,* which is published annually and available to shareholders and other interested parties. A final change can be noted in GM's response to a second set of resolutions submitted by Campaign GM. Three resolutions were submitted for the 1971 proxy statement, which GM accepted for inclusion without comment.

These changes and others that were made during the next few years significantly increased the variety of perspectives included in top management and on the board of directors. As the firm expanded in this manner, it began to better match the variety in its environment. As a result, GM was better able to understand the perspectives of its constituents and the nature of changes taking place in its environment. Burck (1978: 100) noted:

16. See Longstreth and Rosenbloom (1973) for a discussion of the comments submitted to GM by the institutional investors.

Indeed, a case can be made that GM has passed through one of the major turning points of its history. One authority who holds this view is Eugene E. Jennings, professor of Management at Michigan State University, a consultant to top executives of numerous American corporations and a close observer of GM for more than twenty years. "In the late 1960s and early 1970s, GM was one of the most insular and inner-directed companies anywhere," he says. "Now, more than any other company in the auto business, and more than most companies anywhere . . . it has learned how to be outer-directed and strategic—to use its head rather than trying to use its clout." Jennings thinks those practical managers at GM don't fully realize as yet what they have accomplished—but he predicts that they will within a few years as they see the results accumulate.

By the end of 1980, it was apparent to GM managers and auto industry observers how the changes differentiated GM from the other firms in the industry.

GM's Response to Environmental Change

While energy did not emerge as a public issue until the 1973-4 Arab oil embargo, it was being discussed in technical and scientific circles during the late 1960s and the early 1970s. During 1971 and 1972 there was growing concern on the part of outside board members that the corporation should gain a better understanding of the emerging energy problem. This concern was furthered by analyses from GM's Chief Economist's Office, which projected a developing U.S. dependency on foreign oil and subsequent higher prices. The board created an energy task force in July, 1972, composed of individuals from manufacturing, economics, finance, research, design, engineering, and government-industry relations staffs. Its goal was to determine the extent to which an energy problem existed, whether the federal government had a plan for dealing with it, and what its potential impact would be on General Motors' operations. The task force reported back to the board in 1973 with three findings: 1) there was indeed an emerging problem; 2) the government had no plan for dealing with it; and 3) it would have a profound effect on the corporation. The task force was then assigned the task of examining GM's product program in light of its findings.

The task force report generated considerable discussion within the firm. The energy issue emerged a number of times at various high level management meetings and was evident in the April, 1973, ten year product plan presented to top management. Given that managers within the corporation were coming to believe that fuel prices would increase and fuel economy would become a saleable feature in the future, much of the discussion concerned the fuel economy of GM's full-size cars.

The April presentations were important in a number of respects. It was the first move from a five to ten year product plan, reflecting a shift on the part of management toward a longer product-planning horizon. A decision was also reached to reduce the weight of full-size vehicles for the 1977 model year by a target of four hundred pounds, which would increase their fuel economy by about one mile per gallon. This decision was significant in that it was the first conscious effort to reduce vehicle weight, which had been steadily increasing through the 1960s. It also marked the first time that a fuel economy target was included in vehicle design criteria, something GM soon adopted for all its vehicle design efforts.

Management also decided to adopt the project center concept as a device to facilitate the coordination of divisional efforts to meet the weight reduction target.[17] The project center is a temporary unit set up within the corporation as design or component problems common to the five automotive divisions emerge. A project center is staffed by engineers from the automotive divisions, components division, and the corporate engineering and design staffs, as well as other interested parties (e.g., consumer, marketing, and design specialists), who are housed in a single location. A project center staff reports to a board composed of the chief engineers of the automotive divisions, who in turn report to the Corporate Product Policy Group (Burck, 1978). The net effect of the project center concept was that the design process was significantly streamlined since all the parties involved from the various divisions and staffs were working together. Thus, decisions about product design could be made more quickly and efficiently.

In October, 1973, the energy task force presented its recommendations to the board concerning GM's products. The task force recommended that, in light of the potential energy problem, GM should begin downsizing its products to increase fuel economy. Within a matter of weeks, the Arab oil embargo began and the sales of larger vehicles declined precipitously. While the energy task force had not made specific recommendations concerning product changes, it had put top management in the right frame of mind to think about and act on the implications of increasing gasoline prices on GM's operations. As a result, they were able to move quickly with revisions in GM's product program once the embargo began.

17. The project center is a coordination device pioneered by the aerospace industry during the 1960s. It has since been adopted by many firms facing complex design and engineering tasks. The concept was brought to the attention of GM by R. L. Terrell, who had headed one of GM's nonautomotive divisions, Delco Electronics. Terrell spotted the technique while Delco was a NASA subcontractor for the space program (Burck, 1978.)

October through December, 1973, were important months at General Motors. A number of critical decisions were made about products to be offered in the 1975 model year and beyond. In light of the oil embargo, the Product Policy Committee reassessed the ten year product plan and decided that it needed substantial revision. The major change was increasing the weight reduction target for 1977 full-size vehicles to 800-1000 pounds, up from the 400 pound target set in April. The increased weight reductions were projected to increase the fuel economy of 1977 full-size models by three miles per gallon.

On December 21, 1973, the Executive Committee of the board met to review and discuss the 1975, 1976, and 1977 model year small-car programs. Earlier that year, GM began planning for its first small front wheel drive vehicle in conjunction with Opel. With the onset of the embargo, executives decided that it was essential that the corporation offer a competitor to the imports more quickly than originally planned. "Crash" programs were considered and proposals finalized for two new small cars to be introduced in the 1976 model year. The first proposed vehicle was to replace the ill-fated Chevrolet Vega, which had encountered problems with the durability of its engine. Instead of continuing with the plan for a new small front wheel drive vehicle, it was proposed that the corporation engage in a "crash" program to bring out a replacement in eighteen months. The resulting product, the Chevette, was based on an Opel-designed vehicle then being introduced in Brazil. This was GM's first experience with the emerging world vehicle concept.[18] The second "crash" program was for a luxury compact to be marketed by the Cadillac Division. The vehicle, named the Seville, was to compete in the Mercedes-class market segment. In both cases, the proposals to produce the vehicles and the planned market introduction dates were about eighteen months apart. This made them the shortest lead times for the production of new vehicles in the post war years. It cut the usual design and tooling lead time in half.

Two other sets of proposals were discussed at the meeting. The first concerned the development of compact vehicles for the Oldsmobile, Buick, and Pontiac divisions for the 1975 model year. The dealer bodies of these divisions were particularly hard hit by the embargo since they had little to offer in the way of small cars. A decision was also reached to approve the Product Policy Committee's recommendation that the

18. During the late 1970s, GM offered variations of this T-car design world-wide through Chevrolet, Vauxhall, GM do Brasil, Opel, Holden, and Isuzu. All share the same basic design with each specific vehicle's characteristics adapted to suit each country's particular requirements (General Motors Corporation, 1980).

weight reduction target for downsizing the 1977 full-size lines be reset at 800-1000 pounds. The proposals for the Seville and the Chevette were officially approved at an Executive Committee meeting on January 23, 1974. The decision to build compact vehicles for Oldsmobile, Buick, and Pontiac was made in the following month.

General Motors had, during these few months, committed itself to reversing the direction it had maintained since 1946. Instead of building vehicles that grew continually larger, the corporation committed itself to producing smaller, more fuel efficient vehicles to meet the challenge of the energy-constricted 1980s. This new direction was reflected in GM products beginning in the 1976 model year with the introduction of the Chevette and the Seville. In the 1977 model year, smaller full-size vehicles were introduced. They were 700 pounds lighter than their predecessors and achieved about three miles per gallon better fuel efficiency while maintaining the same amount of interior space. Down-sized intermediates were introduced in the 1978 model year with an average weight reduction of 600 pounds and a fuel economy improvement of about three miles per gallon. Full-size luxury vehicles with front wheel drive were introduced during the 1979 model year. These models had an average weight reduction of 1000 pounds and fuel economy improvements of four miles per gallon over their predecessors. In mid-1979, GM began introducing the first of its newly designed vehicles with the 1980 "X-cars," which replaced its existing compacts. The X-car program, initiated in February, 1975, cost the corporation $2.7 billion (Burck, 1979), making it the most expensive design effort in GM's history. Adoption of transverse front wheel drive and other innovations resulted in a weight reduction of 800 pounds and six miles per gallon better fuel economy than the models it replaced.

In recognition of the internationalization of the automotive industry, GM began to reorganize its international operations in 1977. The corporation's foreign subsidiaries were consolidated into the Overseas Operations Group and the managing directors of these subsidiaries were elevated to the level of corporate vice president. The overseas head-quarters was moved to Detroit from New York in 1978, allowing for closer coordination with the corporation's North American operations. GM's first international project center was set up in 1977 with the goal of harmonizing basic designs across national boundaries for a new model world vehicle. Over 20 percent of GM's planned capital investment for the first five years of the 1980s was committed to building new facilities throughout the world. The explicit goal of the integration of its operations was to make GM a stronger international competitor in the emerging global market.

In short, GM downsized its entire product line of domestic passenger vehicles over a five year period and moved to become a truly global competitor. Domestically, GM maintained its share of sales in the face of strong import competition during 1979 and 1980 while Chrysler's and Ford's shares continued to erode. Beginning with the introduction of its new subcompact "J-cars" in May, 1981, GM planned to bring out a new product approximately every six months during the following three years. By the time the 1985 fuel economy standards are effective, GM will have brought out its second generation fleet of fuel efficient vehicles. The transformation was significant, particularly in light of the fact that GM had the largest cars and poorest fuel economy of the automakers only a decade earlier. Internationally, the company became more competitive. It entered the 1980s with an efficient international organization and products that will be competitive in the world market.

Ford Motor Company

During the early 1970s, the biggest problems Ford's managers saw facing the company in the U.S. market were a lack of plant and materials to meet consumer demand and declining profit margins on sales. Profits were lower at Ford, in part, because its major strength was in the less profitable segments of the passenger vehicle market. Ford's domestic strategy in the early 1970s was directed toward increasing profitability by: 1) increasing sales of full-size and luxury vehicles; 2) pushing the company into the profitable semi-luxury field while keeping its small cars loaded with options; 3) increasing its already profitable international operations; and 4) bolstering its profitable truck operations. Lee Iacocca, Ford's president, summed up the intent of the strategy in noting that "we've got to keep up our profit margins" ("Ford in the Future," 1971: 24).

Ford was not particularly interested in venturing into the small-car market any more than it already had since margins on small cars were considerably less than those for larger vehicles. *Forbes* reported in 1971 that, "indeed, the focus on profitability is so intense that Ford has virtually abandoned plans to build a sub-subcompact for the U.S. market." Henry Ford II, Ford's chairman, said, "I don't think we could get enough out of it to make it worth our while" ("Ford in the Future," 1971:24).

The company was in the process of designing its 1976 models when the oil embargo began in October, 1973. Confusion abounded and Henry Ford II became very conservative with regard to the firm's product plans. Despite the urging of Iacocca and Howard Sperlich, vice president for car operations, to concentrate on designing and building smaller vehicles, Ford cut forward product spending by about $2 billion. Instead of working on new vehicle designs, the company focused on restyling existing models for the 1976 model year. Later, Iacocca convinced Ford that the company should build a front wheel drive subcompact for the 1978 model year. The project was scratched by Henry Ford when the company posted a loss during the first quarter of 1975 (Meadows, 1980).

While Ford knew by 1975 that GM was planning to downsize its fleet, he refused to follow suit. There were probably a number of reasons for this. Ford's executives viewed the interruption in the supply of oil and rising gasoline prices triggered by the embargo as an aberration. They expected consumer preferences to shift back to larger vehicles and remain there. This was reinforced when the market began shifting back toward larger vehicles through 1975 and small-car sales rapidly dropped off. Henry Ford also believed that the American public wanted the comfort and prestige traditionally associated with large cars. Also significant was Ford's belief that the company could not earn enough of a profit on small vehicles to offset the tremendous cost of downsizing. When the company was forced to begin downsizing by the passage of the Energy Policy and Conservation Act of 1975, it embarked on a different tack than did GM. Ford, being convinced Americans still wanted large cars, set out to reduce fuel consumption while retaining the large-car look.

When GM introduced its smaller 1977 full-size vehicles in the fall of 1976, the relative position in vehicle size between Ford and GM was reversed. GM had offered the biggest cars in 1973; Ford offered the biggest models across product lines for 1977. Ford focused on the size of its vehicles as a major selling point. The news media were introduced to the new cars by Ford executives who proclaimed, "We sell the biggest ones in town" (*Automotive News*, September 27, 1976: 32). Advertising also focused on size in an attempt to draw business away from the downsized GM products. An ad introducing the 1977 Ford LTD said, for example, "For 1977 some car makers offer you only shorter, narrower, lighter full-size cars . . . Ford has a better idea . . . Ford offers you a choice: Ford LTD. The full-size car that kept its size."

Management at Ford was faced with crisis during 1976 when Henry Ford II was hospitalized with a heart ailment. Questions arose as to who would succeed Ford when he stepped down from the chief executive officer and chairman positions, which he had filled for thirty years. After a period of recuperation, Ford began to reorganize top management with the intent of smoothing the transition when he did decide to step down.

The 1977 reorganization resulted in the creation of the Office of the Chief Executive, which included Lee Iacocca as chief operating officer, Phillip Caldwell as vice chairman, and Ford as chairman and chief executive officer. Although responsibility for the company was shared equally by the three executives, Ford remained firmly in control. In case of disagreement among the three, he would make the final decision ("A New Look At Ford," 1977).

The company began to introduce its downsized vehicles in 1977 as the fuel economy standards went into effect with the 1978 models. The Ford downsizing plan focused first on the low volume small cars with reductions coming for larger vehicles in later years. For the 1978 model year, Ford introduced the Ford Fairmont and the Mercury Zephyr, which replaced the aging Maverick and the Comet. The Fiesta, a subcompact manufactured in Spain, was also introduced to provide Ford with a competitor to the imports and GM's Chevette. Iacocca pushed for domestic production of Fiestas, an idea which Henry Ford vetoed. Reductions were to follow for full-size vehicles in the 1979 model year and 1980 luxury models. It is important to note that these downsized vehicles were considerably larger than the GM vehicles in the same product classification. The compact Ford Fairmont, for example, was approximately the same size as the downsized GM intermediates.

This created a potential problem in that it made it difficult to meet future fuel economy standards. Much of Ford's hope rested on a newly designed subcompact to be introduced in the 1981 model year. The situation was aggravated by the fact that the United Auto Workers, worried about the loss of jobs to captive imports, successfully lobbied for the passage of a law which required 75 percent local content for cars counted in the corporate average fuel economy calculations, effective in 1980. This eliminated the Fiesta, Ford's best mileage car, from the fuel economy calculations after 1979. In 1978, Henry Ford said of the new subcompact, "Everything hangs on the success of that car—it sure does, it has to do *everything* by itself for 1981 and 1982. We'll have to sell every one we make to meet the fuel requirements, and support the profitable end of the line" (Guzzardi, 1978: 42). In July, 1978, Ford abruptly fired Lee Iacocca.

Ford introduced its 1979 full-size vehicles, on which it had spent over a billion dollars to downsize, in late 1978. They were equipped with V-8 engines and had lower fuel economy ratings than their GM counterparts. The introduction came a few months before the auto market slumped in the face of rapidly rising gasoline prices. The results were disastrous. Sales of Ford's intermediate, full-size, and luxury vehicles dropped precipitously. Between January, 1979, and April, 1980, for example, sales of the Lincoln Versailles slipped 63 percent, Mercury Monarch—50 percent, Lincoln Continental—55 percent, Ford Thunderbird—47 percent, and Cougar XR-7—63 percent (Meadows, 1980). The firm cut production drastically as total market volume declined to reduce inventories. The sum result of the year was that Ford lost about 2.5 percent of its market share, primarily to the imports. The company posted a profit based on the strength of its overseas sales. In August 1979, Henry Ford stepped down as chief executive officer, and Phillip Caldwell was appointed to the post. Ford remained chairman of the corporation.

The sales downturn continued into 1980 as the auto industry continued to close plants and lay off employees to cut costs. Henry Ford resigned as chairman in March, 1980, leaving the company without a Ford at the helm for the first time in its history. The financial situation of the firm that Ford turned over to Caldwell, the new chairman, grew worse throughout the year. In the face of the first predicted full-year loss in Ford's post war history, the company announced that it was cutting 1980-4 capital spending by $2.5 billion, from $4 billion annually to $3.5 billion. The move was widely criticized on Wall Street. "The analysts' implications were clear: Without massive effort to redesign what they described as the least competitive product line among the Big Three, Ford faced a future as bleak as its current year" ("Ford Shifts Gears...," 1980: 1C).

Throughout the year, Ford executives continued to pin their hopes on the October, 1980, introduction of its new front wheel drive subcompact, which was developed at a cost of $3 billion. The new vehicle, code named "Erica," was to replace the Ford Pinto and the Mercury Bobcat, which were a decade old and had encountered significant consumer resistance after some highly publicized safety problems. While executives had high hopes for the Erica (Ford Escort and Mercury Lynx), the vehicles simply made Ford competitive with the other automakers in the compact and subcompact fields. Its competitors included the Japanese imports (primarily Toyota, Datsun, and Honda), the Chrysler K-cars introduced at the same time, and the GM J-cars which were later introduced in May, 1981. The year ended with Ford posting a $1.5 billion loss and a second consecutive annual decline in share of sales in the domestic market. The irony was that this occurred even though Ford was the most internationalized manufacturer and had just completed an integration of its world-wide operations outside of North America.

Chrysler Corporation

Chrysler Corporation's problems were somewhat different than those of Ford and General Motors. Chrysler was a large industrial firm by any standards but those used to measure the size of auto companies. It was only a marginal competitor with Ford and GM. Chrysler's sales during the 1950s and 1960s averaged about half of Ford's and one quarter of GM's. Profit margins had also been smaller because of the lower volume over which to spread development costs and the concentration of its volume in the lower end of the market. Chrysler earned 2 cents per dollar of sales in 1973, for example, as compared to Ford's earnings of about 5 cents per dollar and GM's 7 cents per dollar ("What's Wrong at Chrysler?" 1973). The corporation was also more heavily leveraged than its competitors, which made Chrysler vulnerable to swings in the demand for automotive products. In 1973, Chrysler had 37 cents of long-term debt for every dollar of equity, compared to 19 cents per dollar for Ford and 6 cents per dollar at GM ("What's Wrong at Chrysler?" 1973). As a result, Chrysler's earnings were more sensitive to general economic conditions than were those of its competitors.

Unlike its competitors, Chrysler had no cohesive image of itself as an automotive producer to guide its product decisions (Vanderwicken, 1975). Henry Ford I had set the direction of his company with his maxim, "An inexpensive car for the masses." Similarly, Alfred P. Sloan set the tone for GM in the 1920s by visualizing GM as producing "a car for every purse and purpose." Chrysler, on the other hand, inherited a heritage of engineering from Walter P. Chrysler, who built the auto company around his new high compression engine in the 1920s. Vanderwicken (1975) noted that the centrality of engineering never changed. As a result, Chrysler's image of what kind of company it was offered no guidance as to what it should be doing and what types of products it should be offering.

The strategy that the firm pursued under the leadership of Lynn Townsend during the 1960s was one of imitating its competitors as a full line automotive manufacturer. Townsend, an accountant, was noted for his ability to cut costs in response to declining profit margins. His ability in engineering Chrysler's 1961 turnaround had, in fact, won him the confidence of the board and his appointment as president in 1962 and chairman in 1967. During the 1960s, Townsend imitated the competition internationally by building or buying plants in Europe, South America, South Africa, and Australia. Most of these were marginal operations when Chrysler acquired them. Domestically, he attempted to match Ford and GM, product line by product line. Overall, this strategy sapped the firm of much of its strength. Schuyten (1978: 55) noted that "at one point, the company was running marginal or losing operations on every continent except Antartica." Faltering international operations and the attempt to compete with Ford and GM line by line in the U.S. resulted in minimal reinvestment in aging plant and equipment and in the renewal of dated product designs.

In 1970, Chrysler posted the first of a series of losses for the 1970s. GM and Ford were introducing their new subcompacts, the Vega and the Pinto. Chrysler had one on the drawing board, code named the "25," which was to be introduced in 1971. In light of the 1970 loss, plans for the vehicle were scrapped in favor of concentrating on redesigning the firm's full-size vehicles, the sales of which had been declining during the late 1960s. Chrysler executives counted on their aging Valiants and Darts, the last survivors of the 1960 model year compacts, to keep them positioned in the lower end of the market, and that their captive imports would keep the company from being excluded from the growing sub-compact market segment.

As demand for automotive products increased through 1973, the operational problems Chrysler managers faced were the same as else-where in the industry, shrinking profit margins and a lack of plant and material to meet consumer demand. Chrysler was caught off guard by the oil embargo in October, 1973, and reacted with confusion and disbe-lief. The Chrysler management team, for example, did not understand the implications of tighter supplies of energy and higher gasoline costs on consumer demand. A month after the embargo began and automotive sales started declining, Townsend expressed his perspective in stating, "The subcompacts are just too small: The American people just won't climb into them. They have to give up too much in creature comfort. I think that probably the most popular car size you'll see fifteen years from today will be like our intermediates today. But you're still going to see a hell of a lot of big ones around" ("What's Wrong at Chrysler?" 1973: 28).

Chrysler introduced its redesigned 1974 full-size vehicles as the demand for large vehicles declined and compacts and subcompacts increased their market penetration. Chrysler's sales of its aging com-pacts were also depressed as the public turned to the newer vehicles offered by Ford, GM, and the imports. As 1974 began, the company faced three major problems: 1) a $200 million debt acquired in redesigning its full-size vehicles that weren't selling, 2) an aging fleet of compacts, and 3) no domestic subcompact. The firm began to flounder. *Forbes* ("What's Wrong at Chrysler?" 1973: 28-32) called it "a company with products, plants, and money, but with no firm sense of direction. . . . This [management] team has yet to address itself to the basic question every successful company must answer: Who and what are we? If not a full line producer, then what?" As the company moved toward a $52 million loss for 1974, another cost cutting program was undertaken. Plants were closed and workers laid off to reduce inventory. Thousands of engineers and designers were also fired or laid off in an effort to reduce overhead. The effect of this last move was to preserve cash in the short run, but it severely damaged future Chrysler product programs. New car introductions for the next four years ran from four to eight months late.

In mid-1975, Townsend stepped down as chairman and was replaced by John Riccardo, who had been president of the firm. The company that Townsend turned over to Riccardo was in serious financial shape, on the verge of posting a $260 million loss for the year. One of Riccardo's first actions was to initiate the dismantling of Chrysler's global operations. Beginning in 1975 and continuing through the end of the decade, the corporation sold or restructured the ownership of all its global operations. Although this provided needed cash, it put Chrysler in the position of becoming a national automotive company as the market was becoming increasingly international. In the fall of 1975, the aged Dart and the Valiant were retired by the introduction of the Volare and the Aspen. The timing of the introduction was unfortunate in that the new compacts were introduced as the demand for small cars contracted and that for larger vehicles rebounded. The vehicles had been pushed into production in a delayed response to the oil embargo. The speed up and the layoff of engineers and designers led to a number of quality problems, making them two of the most recalled cars in history ("Detroit's Uphill Battle," 1980).

By the end of 1976, Riccardo and Eugene Cafiero, the new president, had completed a strategic plan which was to carry the corporation into the 1980s. It called for a downsizing program which would place Chrysler products within reach of Ford and GM by 1982. New, smaller full-size models would be introduced for the model year 1979, followed by new intermediates in 1980. A new compact to replace the Volare and the Aspen was to be introduced in the 1981 model year, and redesigned vans and pickups were to follow for 1982. The plan called for gutting the plants in which the new vehicles would be built and refitting them with highly automated assembly techniques. The projected cost of the plan in 1976 totaled $7.5 billion (Schuyten, 1978).

In January, 1978, Chrysler introduced its entries into the subcompact field, the Omni and the Horizon, which had been jointly designed with Chrysler's French subsidiary, Simca. The innovative vehicles incorporated front wheel drive and a transverse-mounted four cylinder engine, which provided more passenger space than other compacts on the market. The cars quickly became popular and were named *Motor Trend's* "car of the year." A few months later, *Consumer Reports* published a highly controversial report that the vehicles were unsafe due to a faulty steering system. Although the government and other automakers came to Chrysler's defense, sales declined rapidly, contributing substantially to the $206 million loss the firm reported for 1978.

In November, Lee Iacocca was hired as president of the firm. Iacocca's appointment buoyed the spirits of Chrysler's managers, dealers, and shareholders, who expected him to return the firm to profitability. Over the following few months, Iacocca launched a major reorganization of Chrysler's operations, which brought its structure more in line with that of Ford and General Motors. Operating control was placed more closely in the hands of the divisions and the images of the divisions' products were more clearly differentiated. At about the same time, the company embarked on an advertising campaign to introduce its new full-size vehicles, the St. Regis and the New Yorker. The ads drew customers into dealer showrooms but the vehicles were not there to meet them. The vehicles were delivered late due to production delays. By the time the dealerships were fully stocked at year end, gas prices had begun to increase and sales of large vehicles plummeted. By February, 1979, Chrysler had a 381-day inventory of full-size vehicles. Sales problems were further aggravated by curtailed production of the Omni and the Horizon, whose sales increased with the rising demand for small vehicles. The problem was caused by a shortage of four cylinder engines, which the firm purchased from Volkswagen. Chrysler did not have a four cylinder production capacity of its own, although an eight cylinder engine plant was in the process of being converted.

It became apparant by mid-year that the firm was faced with a severe cash flow problem which could lead to insolvency unless an infusion of money could be found. Riccardo began lobbying in Washington during June with the intent of making the severity of the automaker's problem known and organizing political support. In August, 1979, Riccardo formally approached the Carter Administration with a plea for one billion dollars in financial aid. Riccardo's position was that the firm's problems were in large part caused by the unequal burden government regulation placed upon it. Since it was the smallest of the Big Three, it had the least capital available to meet regulatory mandates and a smaller volume over which to spread the cost of compliance. Having initiated the effort, Riccardo stepped down from the chairmanship because of failing health and a concern that his association with the former management regime would jeopardize the effort to obtain federal aid. Iacocca was appointed chairman.

After considerable debate and compromise, Chrysler persuaded Congress to pass a $1.5 billion loan guarantee program in December, 1979. The loan guarantees had many strings attached. The legislation stipulated that the corporation, its employees, creditors, suppliers, and the communities in which it was located make significant concessions to increase the likelihood that the firm would survive. The legislation also gave the government considerable leverage in determining the form in which Chrysler would emerge in the future. The plan stipulated that by 1984 the company would produce only front wheel drive cars and trucks, predominantly powered by four cylinder engines. It also required that Chrysler abandon efforts to remain a full line automotive manufacturer, by reducing the number of product lines from five to three. The year closed with Chrysler posting a $1.1 billion loss.

High interest rates, steep gasoline prices, and an economy in recession continued to plague industry sales during 1980. Chrysler's new 1980 model intermediates were met with indifference on the part of consumers, who continued to shop for small, fuel efficient cars, if they shopped at all. The firm posted a loss in each of the first two quarters as sales continued to decline. July production for the Big Three was at the lowest level in eight years. In August, 1980, Chrysler introduced the long awaited compact "K-car." The attention given the K-cars (Aries and Reliant) during the effort to obtain loan guarantees and the promotion mounted prior to its introduction by the corporation created substantial consumer interest in the vehicle. Sales were good during the following two months but dropped off by mid-fall. Chrysler had miscalculated again. It had loaded the vehicles in dealer showrooms with options in an attempt to increase the profit margin per vehicle and improve the company's cash flow ("Distress That Won't Go Away," 1981). The result was that the compact K-car was as expensive as most of the intermediates on the market. While curious customers came to see the vehicle, relatively few purchased it.

As the year ended, Chrysler was negotiating for the next installment of the federal loan guarantee and further restructuring its debt. The $1.7 billion loss recorded for 1980 was the largest ever by an American corporation. With the majority of its loan guarantee package used up and no prediction for significant improvement in economic conditions during 1981, Chrysler's future as an independent entity was very much in doubt.

Variety and Strategic Decision Making

What had transpired in the course of the decade was that the domestic niche in which the automakers operated evolved, reflecting changes in the international environment. Changing consumer demands fueled by rising gas prices, government regulations, and strong import competition rapidly modified the situation in the U.S. which the industry had come to accept as normal during the 1950s and 1960s. General Motors perceived and acted on these changes during the critical early years of the 1970s while Ford and Chrysler did not. By increasing the variety embodied in its structure, GM registered important information about its environment. As a result, the firm was able to quickly reverse its direction by shifting to a program to build a fuel efficient fleet of automotive vehicles both domestically and internationally. GM's timely action left Ford and Chrysler at least two years behind, attempting to catch up.

As was suggested at the beginning of this chapter, simply monitoring the environment does not ensure that an organization will develop adaptive responses to changing constituent preferences and environmental conditions. It is almost certain that at least a few individuals at Ford and Chrysler saw and understood how the automotive environment was changing. The variety captured by an organization has to be preserved in the strategic decision processes in order to increase the likelihood of adaptive behavior. The decision-making processes at GM did preserve this variety. Unlike the other firms in the industry, General Motors has what might be termed an evolutionary decision process. Decisions usually emerge, they are not "made." The management system developed by Alfred P. Sloan, Jr., president from 1923-37 and chairman from 1937-56, is in large part responsible for this. Insiders refer to the system as one of "decentralized operating responsibilities with coordinated policy control" (General Motors Corporation, 1976). Overall principles and objectives are determined by top management; but how they are achieved is left to the discretion of managers in the operating divisions. In simpler terms, GM refers to this philosophy as "giving people a clear cut job to do and letting them do it."

The concern here is with the GM policy-setting apparatus which operates at the corporate level. Policy is formulated and decisions made through the committee system. There are a number of policy groups, which consider policy suggestions and recommendations from the staff and line organizations as well as from other sources such as the board of directors and its committees. These groups draft proposals and make recommendations to the Executive Committee, which makes the final policy decisions. The policy groups are composed of divisional and corporate executives concerned with the area and issues within a policy group's domain. At the critical meetings of the Engineering Policy Group in December, 1973, for example, where proposals were formulated as to what vehicles GM should produce in the future, there were a variety of line and staff representatives. Corporate interests were represented by executives from the Engineering, Operations, Manufacturing, Financial, Industry-Government Relations, Public Relations, Design, and Environmental Activities staffs. Operating divisions were represented by group executives for the Body and Assembly, Overseas Operations, Car and Truck, Automotive, and Non-Automotive and Defense groups.[19] In short, policy groups are composed of many interested parties, who bring a variety of perspectives to bear on the issues before each group.

Decisions are not made in the policy group meetings. Rather, they are arrived at through informal discussions leading to an emerging consensus. The consensus is ratified at the formal meetings and communicated to the Executive Committee. Quinn (1978: 8-9) noted that "it is difficult to pinpoint the precise time when these 'decisions' [about products during October–December, 1973]—or many other major decisions—in General Motors were actually made. Well prior to the presentation of matters at formal sessions of GM's governing committees and policy groups, a broad consensus is generally obtained among members of senior management. Part of this occurs as members of the executive committee sit along with other key staff and operating executives on various policy groups—subcommittees of the executive committee—where important topics are discussed. In addition, all top executives receive continuing input on significant matters from varied levels of the organization outside of the formal policy group meetings." The formal meetings are, according to Elliot M. Estes, GM president from 1974-81,

19. Information from GM internal documents.

more "for confirmation and communication of a decision than for deliberation" (Burck, 1981: 51). They provide an opportunity for all the interested parties to state their remaining concerns as the groups arrive at a formal consensus. This consensus building approximates what Rittel and Weber (1973: 162) saw as the appropriate way to approach a wicked problem: "an argumentative process in the course of which an image of the problem and of the solution emerges gradually among the participants, as a product of incessant judgment, subject to critical argument."

Ford's and Chrysler's policy systems contained much less variety. Low variety policy and decision systems are appropriate in situations where the environment of an organization is stable. They become inappropriate as an organization's environment changes, because they tend not to register information about changing environmental conditions and constituent preferences. As a result, changing conditions are often not taken into account in formulating strategic policy, which can have disastrous impact on the organization. At both Ford and Chrysler, the major voices in policy making during the early 1970s were those of the chairmen of their respective boards, Henry Ford and Lynn Townsend.

Ford Motor Company had adopted the decentralized management system developed by GM after Henry Ford II took control of the company from his grandfather at the end of World War II. Divisions had a fair degree of autonomy and a committee system was devised for policy making. As Ford put it, "We have committees for everything and all our decisions are studied by the appropriate committees" ("Henry Ford is Still the Boss," 1977: 25). Although the form of the process was the same as GM's, the substance was very different. Henry Ford made the decisions. Ford was characterized by one industry observer as "a very public figure, he cut a swath through high society yet was the unquestioned authority at Ford who could—and did—sack top executives or command product changes on the spot ("Ford's Hot Seat," 1980: 24). His control of the company was unquestioned. There are reports (which Ford denies) that he settled an argument at least on one occasion in saying, "Gentlemen, it is my name on the building" ("Ford and the Future," 1971). Ford also accepted the responsibility for making the decision not to promptly downsize Ford's fleet in the wake of the oil embargo. He said, in 1978, "We sat around here gritting our teeth knowing that GM was downsizing its big cars. I take full responsibility for the decision not to. But I thought it wasn't right for us to overextend ourselves" (Guzzardi, 1978: 42). Townsend's role at Chrysler was similar. In a review of Chrysler's problems, Schuyten (1978: 55) characterized him as "more like a Hollywood czar than a midwestern auto company chief. He was a handsome and dictatorial leader who enjoyed a high reputation as a numbers man, but he never really seemed to understand the fundamental business of his company." Schuyten (1978: 56) also noted that "Townsend was said to be in so much of a habit of countermanding his executives' decisions that nobody was accustomed to responsibility."

The point is that the strategic systems at Ford and Chrysler did not register information about how the firms' domestic and international niches were changing. As a result, important information was not included in the formulation of strategic policy. The chairmen who set policy had only a limited perspective, and it was not one sensitive to changing environmental conditions. The strategies Ford and Chrysler pursued reflected this to their detriment. The policy system at GM, in contrast, was variety rich. It registered information about changing conditions and preserved it as policy was being formulated. As a result, the organization increased the likelihood of selecting an adaptive course for the future. GM's performance was more effective than that of Ford or Chrysler, in that its performance evolved as its niche evolved.

6
Implications for Evaluation and Managerial Practice

Both case studies show that organizations need to gauge and respond to constituent preferences for performance as well as be aware of the constraints which bound that performance. Changes in either constraints or preferences can change the degree to which an organization is performing effectively. Those organizations which satisfy preferences for performance over time through niche expansion enhance their own and the larger society's adaptability. Increasing adaptability while meeting current preferences is the hallmark of effectiveness from the evolutionary perspective. The implications that can be derived from the physician extender case study are primarily concerned with evaluative practice, while the automotive industry case provides insight into managerial practice.

It was shown in the physician extender case how low variety, goal-based evaluations can place blinders on evaluators and administrators. The goal-based evaluations of the extender training programs did not examine constituent preferences for performance or the effect of environmental constraints on performance. The result was that program evaluators and administrators were blinded to the impact of performance as well as its potential. The evolutionary approach, on the other hand, did provide this type of information, through an examination of performance related to constituent preferences within the context of the constraints in which it was taking place. The contrast between the goal-based and evolutionary approaches lends itself to a number of implications for evaluative practice, which are discussed in the following sections. Three areas are discussed: the evaluative process itself, the selection of constituencies, and the role of the evaluator in the evaluative process.

In the automotive industry case study, it was shown how low

variety evaluative and control mechanisms can prevent organizations from detecting and acting on critical changes in constituent preferences and environmental constraints. The impact of not registering such changes was also shown to have a detrimental effect on organizational adaptability. The implications for managerial action discussed in the following explore two questions. The first concerns the problem of how organizations can satisfy current preferences for performance while increasing future adaptability. The second concerns the relationship between evaluation, decision making, and strategic planning, with an emphasis on the continuity of organizational action within the context of time.

Implications for Evaluative Research

The Evaluative Process

The most commonly employed evaluative approach is the goal-based model. The goal-based model can be characterized as a preordinate evaluative technique (Stake, 1975). It is preordinate in that the goals to be assessed are preordained prior to the initiation of the activity being evaluated. The model's primary concern is with the certification of the attainment of goals set by an organization's managers, as opposed to the assessment of the impact of performance in relation to constituent preferences. As such, the goal-based model is not amenable to evaluations embodying a social evolutionary perspective.

Two models in the educational evaluation literature, the responsive and goal-free models, lend themselves to assessing the impact of organizational performance. Both conceptualize the role of evaluation as being more than the assessment of goal attainment. They treat evaluation as a process of discovery in which the full effects of organizational performance are uncovered and examined. In essence, both focus on the impact of performance instead of its intent. Stake (1975: 14) characterized responsive evaluation as being an alternative to preordinate evaluation, which is

based on what people do naturally to evaluate things—they observe and react. . . . [An evaluation] is a responsive evaluation if it orients more directly to program activities than to program intents, responds to audience requirements for information, and if the different value-perspectives present are referred to in reporting the success or failure of the program.

Responsive evaluation's purpose is, therefore, to discover constituent preferences for and reactions to performance. The evaluative process is responsive in that it responds to the interests of an organization's constituencies.

The form of a responsive evaluation is also different than that of a goal-based evaluation. Goal-based evaluations, at their best, attempt to treat organizational performance as a field experiment with appropriate controls, which allows for a determination of whether the organization has achieved its desired outcomes. A responsive evaluation, on the other hand, is more flexible and loosely organized. It focuses on the effects of organizational performance in relation to what organizational constituencies feel is desirable. Stake (1975: 14) described the process as follows:

To do a responsive evaluation, the evaluator conceives of a plan of observations and negotiations. He arranges for persons to observe the program, and with their help prepares brief narratives, portrayals, product displays, graphs, etc. He finds out what is of value to his audiences, and gathers different expressions of worth from various persons whose points of view differ. Of course, he checks the quality of his records; he gets program personnel to react to the accuracy of his portrayal, authority figures to react to the importance of his findings, and audience members to react to the relevance of his findings. He does much of this informally—iterating and keeping a record of action and reaction. He chooses media accessible to his audiences to increase the likelihood and fidelity of communication. He might prepare a final written report, he might not—depending on what he and his clients have agreed on.

Scriven's (1973) concept of goal-free evaluation is similar to Stake's responsive evaluation model but with a different emphasis. Scriven's model is similar to Stake's in that the purpose of a goal-free evaluation is the discovery of the effects of an organization's performance. It does not matter whether these are intended or unintended effects. Both have an impact on an organization's constituencies. Scriven noted that the goal-free approach does not penalize an organization for failing to attain overly ambitious goals. As House (1972) pointed out, many stated organizational goals, particularly those of public sector organizations, are overly ambitious. They have to be in order for the organizations to obtain the funding. This often causes problems when an organization does not attain these goals and then attempts to obtain further funding. In a goal-free evaluation, an organization is recognized for its accomplishments. It doesn't matter whether the accomplishments were the intended goals. In fact, many desirable effects of organizational performance often are unintended as are its undesirable effects. Even if an organization is attaining its stated goals only partially, it may be the best performance possible given environmental constraints. The question that the goal-free model raises is whether an organization should be condemned or commended for only partially attaining its goals in such a situation.

The contrast between responsive, goal-free evaluation and preordinate evaluation also points to an interesting question: Do we want to evaluate what people wanted at some particular time in the past or do we want to know how well the organization is satisfying the preferences that people have now? The preferences on which individuals base their judgments of organizational performance are dynamic. Interactions with an organization and changing environmental conditions can foster changes in preferences for organizational performance. Given that preferences change over time, which type of knowledge is more useful to the consumers of an evaluation, an evaluation of performance made using past or present preferences? Preordinate evaluation focuses on the past, responsive, goal-free evaluation on the present.

Beyond the issue of the types of information forthcoming from different evaluative approaches, there is also a question of the effect the evaluative process can have on organizational action. Pondy (1977a) noted that preordinate evaluative processes are directed toward convergent control of a system. This is to say that they focus on making actions within an organization conform to a predetermined course. Similarly, Scriven (1973) noted that evaluators employing a preordinate approach try to "lock" an organization's performance into place. Otherwise, they cannot tell what has produced the effects being examined. This, in turn, discourages creativity and attempts to change an organization's performance to adjust to changing constituent preferences and environmental constraints. In contrast, goal-free, responsive evaluative processes are oriented toward making sense out of what is occurring in a system (Pondy, 1977a). They are more conducive to innovation since they are not directed toward convergent control of the system. Given that effective performance over time comes about through variations in performance which are niche expanding, an organization needs evaluative mechanisms that allow for deviation away from a prescribed course of action.

From the standpoint of the evolutionary meta criterion, preordinate evaluation discourages the types of behavior that make organizations effective. An organization has to respond to changing constituent preferences and environmental constraints in order to be effective over time.

Preordinate evaluation directs an organization's performance toward what was preferred, not what is preferred. Responsive, goal-free evaluation directs performance toward what is preferred, and at the same time, does not discourage or penalize managers for pursuing innovative courses of action.

Selecting Constituencies

The first step in assessing the impact of performance is selecting constituencies to be included in the evaluation. Although there are no cut-and-dry methods of specifying which constituencies to include in an evaluation, there are a number of guidelines that can help in the task of selection. The obvious constituencies of an organization are easy to identify. Most organizations will have managers, employees, customers/clients, suppliers, creditors, owner/stockholders, and so on. These constituencies present no problem. It is important that the evaluator also consider constituencies who are not as prominent as those above, but who may have an important impact on the organization or vice versa. Some of these constituencies may be latent. Consider the case of the tobacco industry. Nonsmokers were a constituency that was nonobvious and latent for a long period (Miles and Cameron, 1982). Until recently, they had not been organized. But, over the past decade, they have had an impact on the industry through their efforts to enact legislation to ban smoking in public places.

Its also important to keep in mind that the composition of a constituency can change. Purcell and Cavanagh (1972), for example, documented the changes in the composition of employees in a number of companies manufacturing small electrical appliances. What had once been a white, middle-income work force was radically transformed into a minority labor force during the 1960s. The new employees had a different conception of the nature of work and a new set of performance preferences. Qualitative changes in the membership of a constituency will have an impact on constituent expectations for performance.

The composition of an organization's pool of constituencies will also change over time. Old constituencies may withdraw; new ones may appear as the salience of an organization's performance to them changes (March and Olson, 1976). The relative importance of different constituencies may also change over time. In the physician extender case, third-party insurers occupied a prominent position in relation to program performance through the 1970s. As third-party insurers accept extenders as bona fide providers of medical care and reimburse for their services as a matter of course, their importance as a constituency of the training programs is likely to decline while other constituencies emerge as more important.

The dynamic nature of the composition of the pool of organizational constituencies is important in two ways. First, an organization needs to be aware of and adjust to changes in its constituencies. Changes in an organization's constituencies require modifications in organizational performance to satisfy new preferences. What was once effective performance may not be under the new criteria imposed by new or changed constituencies. Second, evaluators need to reassess periodically the composition of the pool of constituencies that they have selected for an evaluation. They should not be lulled into a false sense of security that once they have identified constituencies they will be the same at some later time, or that their preferences will be stable.

One way of identifying specific constituencies is through a snow-balling interview technique (Walton, 1971). Evaluators start with the most obvious constituencies (e.g., managers and employees) and ask them who they interact with. They would then interview these "nominated" persons and ask them who else they perceive as affecting or being affected by the organization's performance. An evaluator should be able to arrive at a fairly complete inventory of constituencies for a given period of time through this type of process. Evaluators often cannot assess all an organization's constituencies' preferences and judgments of effectiveness because of limitations of time and money. In this situation, they must take steps to insure that the variety of constituent preferences is adequately represented in the evaluation. Evaluators want to preserve variety in a quantitative sense (the number of constituencies), but more importantly, they want an accurate pattern of variety (i.e., representation of the constituent perspectives). One method for attempting to ensure an accurate pattern of variety is through sampling. The process would begin by selecting one constituency and then identifying another whose perspective on organizational performance lies in opposition to it. This second constituency should be included in the sample and another in opposition to it be identified. The evaluator should continue selecting constituencies in this manner until the overlapping of value perspectives of the remaining constituencies becomes redundant. In the final analysis, the selection of constituencies is a judgmental task and beyond the reach of social science methodology (Stake, 1967). It is, therefore, important that the evaluator report the selection procedure employed.

The Role of the Evaluator

The primary goal of an evaluator is to create an "appreciation" of the relationship between constituent preferences for and the constraints on organizational performance. In doing this, an evaluator creates a situation in which the participants can begin to define effective performance. Vickers (1965: 40) noted:

> An appreciation involves making judgments of fact about the 'state of a system,' both internally and in its external relations. I will call these reality judgments. These include judgments about what the state will be or might be on various hypotheses as well as judgments of what is and has been. They may thus be actual or hypothetical, past, present, or future. It also involves making judgments about the significance of these facts to the appreciator or to the body for whom the appreciation is made. These judgments I will call value judgments. . . . The relation between judgments of fact and of value is close and mutual; for facts are relevant only in relation to some judgment of value and judgments of value are operative only in relation to some configuration of fact.

An appreciation is directed toward creating an understanding of the whole rather than of the individual elements of the system. It is a description of the state of the system in terms of both fact and value. An appreciation is not an analytical concept; it is analogic. It is a synthesis of the constituencies' complementary perspectives on organizational performance into a holistic image of the impact of organizational performance.

An appreciation of organizational effectiveness cannot be stated in the usual manner of saying that an organization has been effective or ineffective. The whole concept is too complex to be reduced to a few words or numbers. The appreciation itself has to be communicated. Evaluators have to communicate their understanding of the relationship between an organization's performance, environmental constraints, and constituent preferences. If a competent job has been done in evaluating and communicating the results of the evaluation, other individuals should be able to derive a similar appreciation.

A good example of a study that created and communicated an appreciation is *The Limits to Growth,* by Meadows et al. (1972). They reported the results of a computer simulation designed to investigate five major trends of global concern (i.e., accelerating industrialization, rapid population growth, widespread malnutrition, depletion of nonrenewable resources, and a deteriorating environment) and their potential impact on global society. The findings indicated that if current trends were to continue unchecked, human society would collapse by the year 2100. The importance of the book lies in the appreciation it generated for those who read it. It created an understanding of the trends, ecological constraints, their interactions, and the potential outcomes. *The Limits to Growth* communicated something more than the sum of the individual trends. It synthesized the various components into a whole, through which the reader became aware of the individual components, their interaction, and their impact.

Implications for Strategic Behavior

Two implications about strategic behavior can be derived from the auto industry case study.[20] The first concerns balancing demands for stability with demands for change in behavior through performance. Organizations must meet current preferences for performance while creating variations in behavior which enhance their ability to adapt to changing preferences and constraints. Second, the evolutionary model suggests that evaluation, decision making, and strategic planning are not, as they are usually treated, separate activities. Rather, they are complementary aspects of making judgments about performance, having different temporal dimensions. Treating them separately can pit the past and the present against the future.

Increasing Organizational Variety through Strategic Behavior

In a general sense, the evolutionary model specifies that an effective organization creates variations in its behavior for selection into the social system's repertoire. It is necessary to keep in mind that variation and retention work at cross-purposes (Weick, 1977; 1979). If an organization were to devote all its energy toward generating variations, none would be retained and the system would fail. On the other hand, if an organization directed all its energy toward retention, no variations would be available to satisfy changing preferences and meet shifting environmental constraints. Again, the system would fail. It is implicit in

20. A third implication might concern the creation of mechanisms to register and preserve variety within organizational evaluative and decision processes. How to create such mechanisms has been addressed in the extensive literature on organizational design (e.g., Galbraith, 1973; Kilmann, Pondy, and Slevin, 1976; Nystrom and Starbuck, 1980) and organization/environment relations (e.g., Aldrich, 1979; Starbuck, 1976). Interested readers should refer to these sources.

the concept of the evolutionary meta criterion that a balance must exist between variation and retention. As Weick (1977: 207) noted, "Doing what you have always done is necessary for short-term adaptation; doing what you have never done is necessary for long-term adaptation." Weick (1977) and Pondy (1977b) addressed this issue in their discussions on how organizations can enhance long-term adaptability. They also described how a balance between variation and retention can be maintained. Weick (1977) suggested that an organization can increase its potential for long-term adaptation by being (among other things) clumsy, wandering, and hypocritical.

A clumsy organization intentionally complicates or elaborates its pattern of behavior, which separates it somewhat from the attainment of goals. This provides the room for an organization to experiment with the elements of its retained knowledge. Novel reconstructions or elaborations of behavior allow individuals to gain a better understanding of the elements in the existing repertoire. They also provide the potential for discovering new desirable performances. By elaborating or complicating behaviors within the organization's repertoire, variations are introduced into the system which provide potential responses to changing preferences and constraints.

In a more pragmatic vein, this means that organizations need to engage in activities which are not directly related to the attainment of current organizational goals. By decoupling behavior from goals and doing something differently, organizations often create variations which may help them adapt to changing preferences and constraints in the future. At General Motors, for example, engineers and designers had been working on a design for a small luxury vehicle during the early 1970s that was not directly a part of the forward product program. When top management began considering a crash progam to build more fuel efficient vehicles after the onset of the oil embargo, they found that the designers and engineers had already put one together. This allowed the corporation to introduce the Cadillac Seville eighteen months after a decision had been made to build the car. In effect, the designers and engineers increased the adaptability of the organization by creating a novel variation which allowed it to respond to changing preferences and constraints quickly.

Another implication of the clumsy organization is that efficiency may preclude adaptability. The finely tuned organization creates few novel variations in behavior because all its efforts are directed toward attaining current goals. If these goals become inappropriate in the face of changing preferences and constraints, the organization will have a difficult time adapting. Townsend's actions at Chrysler after the oil embargo provide an illustration of the trade-offs between efficiency and adaptability. It became obvious that Chrysler would post a loss for 1974 as sales slumped in the wake of the oil embargo. One of Townsend's reactions was to reduce the loss by lowering overhead expenses. This was accomplished by laying off and firing engineers and designers. The long-run effect of becoming more cost efficient was that it eliminated those individuals who could create novel variations needed to respond to changing preferences and constraints. Clearly, efficiency precluded adaptability in this situation. The central point is that organizations cannot act solely in the context of the present. They have to act with the future in mind. This requires that they create modes of behavior which may be inefficient in today's context but adaptive in the face of the changing preferences and constraints they might encounter in the future.

The concept of a hypocritical organization focuses on the fact that lessons learned from experience become dated as the circumstances in which they were learned change. Since conventional wisdom becomes dated, organizations must accept the equivocal as unequivocal, and vice versa. Another way to characterize this is in terms of Kelly's (1964) notion of the invitational mood. Kelly suggested that it is often useful to suspend disbelief and to approach ideas on the basis of "if this were true, then . . ." This often allows individuals to create novel ideas and insights because they are not bound by conventional wisdom.

The assumptions and beliefs that many auto industry executives had about the supply and price of energy and small cars during the early 1970s is illustrative of the effects of organizational hypocrisy. Executives at GM approached the supply and price of gasoline from the "if this were true" position in examining the potential impact of an energy crisis in 1972. By suspending the conventional assumption about a steady and cheap supply of gasoline, they discovered something novel about their organization's performance. They realized that performance was likely to be very sensitive to shifts in the supply and price of gasoline. While continuing to build large cars, they began designing and engineering vehicles as if there were tight supplies of gasoline. As a result, GM executives were able to react quickly to the developing energy problem because they had already discredited the assumption of cheap and plentiful gasoline.

At Ford and Chrysler, belief in the conventional wisdom slowed their ability to respond to changing preferences and constraints. The major figures in both firms did not believe that the American consumer wanted small cars. Perhaps more importantly, they did not believe small cars could be built profitably. While these beliefs may have been correct under the set of preferences and constraints that defined their niche during the 1950s and 1960s, they quickly lost their validity in the 1970s as conditions changed. Small cars had been less profitable than large cars during the 1960s. But, as gasoline prices increased during the 1970s it became impossible to earn a profit on large vehicles because the auto-makers couldn't sell them. Small cars, therefore, became relatively profitable. Continued belief in the correctness of experiences gained under different business conditions affected their ability to respond to changing conditions. In short, the hypocritical organization is one which doubts what it knows and knows what it doubts. By questioning the certain and accepting the uncertain, organizations can often create the right atmosphere to generate novel variations in behavior which en-hance adaptability.

The notion of a wandering organization focuses on the idea that if an organization does not take the shortest path to attaining a desired end, the process of attaining the end may lead to the discovery of new desirable performances. A wandering organization, in effect, puts the process of attaining an end on a par with its attainment. This explicitly raises the possibility that the process of getting someplace may often be as important as actually getting there. By deviating from the shortest or most efficient path for goal attainment, an organization may discover other ends that are desirable and new ways of attaining them. Where the notion of a clumsy organization focused on the novel recombination of existing elements of behavior, the concept of a wandering organization centers on the complication of the whole process by which desirable ends are attained. In both cases, variations based on elements of cur-rently retained behaviors can be generated.

An example of wandering behavior was provided by General Mo-tors during the early 1970s. As GM came to grips with the idea that supplies of energy would be tighter in the future, it gave one of its designers, Horatio Shakespear, the job of being a "corporate thinker." His assignment was "pondering the company's future and then design-ing cars that will fit into that vision. He has no deadlines and no day-to-day responsibilities" ("Mulling It Over," 1980: 1). Shakespear was, in effect, officially made a wanderer whose task was to examine possible futures and how the corporation might get to them. The end point wasn't a goal; rather, the process of getting to the future was. By decoupling this individual's position from the attainment of current goals, GM created an opportunity to develop novel variations which would potentially increase its adaptability.

Pondy (1977b) raised an important point in noting that Weick (1977) was not talking about random variations in performance. Clumsy, wandering, and hypocritical organizations are introducing *deviations* from the knowledge that they have retained. As such, variations honor tradition by deviating from it. Pondy also noted that in looking at the adaptability of the whole system, it is the variations created by a population of organizations that should be examined.

If all organizations were to choose the same solution for achieving effectiveness, and it turned out to be wrong, then the entire set of organizations would be in trouble. An alternative is to plan ways of achieving effectiveness for the entire collection of organizations. That is, diversity of ways of organizing should characterize the population of organizations, not just each individual organization. (Pondy, 1977b: 233)

In the steel industry example in Chapter 3, various firms responded in different ways to the federal regulations on pollution control. One of these variations, the "bubble concept," had the potential of increasing organization/environment adaptability through niche expansion. It would have been less likely for an adaptive variation to have been created if all the firms had chosen the same behavior for responding to federal regulations. The development of a variety of behaviors in response to changing preferences and constraints is desirable from the perspective of enhancing societal adaptability. Clumsy, hypocritical, and wandering organizations increase adaptability by acting in a manner which enables them simultaneously to balance demands for stability and change. While organizations must act in a manner which satisfies current preferences within the context of existing constraints, they must also create variations in behavior which enable them to respond to future preferences and changing environmental conditions. In short, long-run adaptability of the organization/environment is enhanced by increasing the pool of variations available to meet future demands.

Evaluation, Decision Making, and Strategic Planning

Evaluation, decision making, and strategic planning are usually viewed as three distinct activities. When the dimension of time is added to the analysis, an interesting relationship among the three activities emerges. Viewed within the continuity of time, all three are the same activity. Each is concerned with judgments about organizational action. The only difference is that they have different temporal dimensions. Evaluation is making judgments about past performance; decision making, about present performance; and strategic planning, about future performance.

These activities are treated separately within most organizations, which creates a problem in that the continuity between past, present, and future actions is destroyed. Most managers are concerned with past and present performance; few are concerned with the future. The past is viewed as useful to the degree that it can be used to predict the future. Operations research and management science, for example, make predictions about future states of organizational performance based on historical information. This is a valid exercise only so long as the assumptions underlying past performance do not change. As was suggested by the evolutionary model, change is continual. Performance preferences and the constraints which define an organization's niche are constantly changing. This creates a dangerous situation in that predictions will have little validity if the assumptions on which they are based change over time. In effect, many organizations pit the past and present against the future.

This problem can be minimized if all three activities are viewed as complementary components of the process of making judgments about performance. This would maintain the continuity between evaluation, decision making, and strategic planning. What was once the future becomes the present and eventually recedes into the past. Treating the three as separate entities disrupts the continuity of organizational action and impedes an organization's ability to modify performance to satisfy changing preferences within the context of shifting constraints.

Differences in the strategic decision systems at GM and Ford provide an illustration of the potential impact of separation.[21] A strategic planning function was created within both companies during 1977. GM's strategic planning group appears to fill a complementary role in the corporate policy system while Ford's appears to have an adjunct position. Strategic planning at GM began during the early 1970s, when members of what was eventually to become the strategic planning staff worked with different policy groups and task forces. In 1977, the planner's role was formalized by the creation of the strategic planning group. The strategic planning unit at Ford was set up during the 1977 reorganization, when the Office of the Chief Executive was created as a mechanism to prepare the company for the transition of power that would take place when Henry Ford stepped down. It appears that there had not

---

21. The information about planning at Ford and GM was obtained through interviews with managers and executives.

been any serious attempt at strategic planning prior to the creation of the planning unit.

In keeping with the nature of the policy formulation process at GM, planners have both formal and informal roles. On a formal level, they create strategic plans which present their interpretation of where GM should be at some future point in time. Generally, this is the standard domain of strategic planning. Perhaps more important, members of the strategic planning group meet regularly with corporate executives on an informal basis. The planners see a major part of their corporate role as being one of getting executives to take a longer term perspective in making decisions, to think about the impact of today's decisions on the future that the company will face tomorrow. The effect of the formal and informal activities is to help management design "turbulence proof" strategies. The planners are, in other words, trying to get executives to look at the assumptions they are using in making decisions and to consider the effect that changes in these assumptions would have on future performance. The end result is an attempt to make strategic choices which have the greatest likelihood of being adaptive under the widest variety of possible future conditions. The planners' future focus is integrated into the strategic policy system as complementing the executives' present and past orientations.

The strategic planning function at Ford appears to emphasize the formal aspects of planning much more than that at GM. Planners are charged with plotting out the future of the corporation. The informal side of planning appears to be much less developed than at GM. This configuration has two drawbacks. First, part of the problem with highly formalized plans is that they become dated the day they are issued. Organizations gain experience against which to test a plan's assumptions as what was the future becomes the present and recedes into the past. More often than not, the assumptions used in making a formal plan do not match well with reality since they were predicated on past experience. The informal side of the planning process avoids this to a degree because it is much more fluid. Assumptions about the future are under continual discussion and modified as experience dictates. Second, and perhaps more important, the planning function is separated from the policy-making process. This results in planning playing a limited role in policy formulation and, occasionally, in its exclusion.

An example of this occurred in the late 1970s as Ford executives were discussing whether to incorporate front wheel drive into future vehicle designs. Planners promoted front wheel drive as something that would help meet future product preferences. Executives promoted rear wheel drive because of the corporation's sunk investment in rear wheel drive vehicles. The future orientation ended up competing with the past/present orientation. As one former executive put it, "A great strategic system went to hell" as the policy process got bogged down. The end result was that Ford will be the last domestic automaker to convert to front wheel drive vehicles.

In short, evaluation, decision making, and strategic planning are the same activity with different temporal orientations. Organizations need to treat the three as complementary processes, each with a role in assisting the organization in responding to evolutionary changes in preferences and constraints. Evaluation can provide information about the impact of performance in light of current preferences; decision making modifies performance to meet existing preferences within current constraints; and strategic planning should inform decision makers in judging the relationship of current performance to future preferences within the context of shifting constraints. All three are necessarily interrelated activities.

Conclusion

The conclusion drawn from the evolutionary model is straightforward. Organizational effectiveness is not a known or constant quantity. The substantive nature of effective performance for any organization changes as constituent preferences and the constraints which define an organization's niche change. Effective performance requires that an organization satisfy evolving constituent preferences through niche expansion over time. This increases the adaptability of the organization/environment by making variations available to meet changing social and physical conditions. By performing in such a manner, an organization continually renews the basis of its legitimacy by satisfying the changing needs of individuals who interact with it over time.

In order to accomplish this task, organizations need to develop and maintain evaluative, control, and decisional systems which register and preserve variety. These systems must inform decision makers as to the nature of constituent preferences, the impact of performance in relation to these preferences, and the effect of environmental constraints on performance in satisfying preferences. This requires that organizations focus on the impact of performance as opposed to its intent. Since preferences and constraints change over time, it is necessary that evaluators and managers engage in constant evaluation. Performance that is effective today is equally likely to be ineffective tomorrow as preferences and constraints change. The goal of the effective organization is, continually, to *become* effective rather than *be* effective. The journey is, in this case, more important than the destination.

References

"A New Look at Ford," *Iron Age,* (April 25, 1977): 16.

Alderman, M. A. and Schoenbaum, E. E. "Detection and Treatment of Hypertension at the Work Site," *New England Journal of Medicine, 293* (1975): 65-68.

Aldrich, H. E. *Organizations and Environments.* Englewood Cliffs, N.J.: Prentice-Hall, 1979

Arrow, K. J. *Social Choice and Individual Values.* New York: Wiley, 1951.

Ashby, W. R. *An Introduction to Cybernetics.* London: University Paperbacks, 1956.

✓ Barnard, C. *The Function of the Executive.* Cambridge, Mass.: Harvard University Press, 1938.

Bass, B. M. "Ultimate Criteria of Organizational Worth," *Personnel Psychology, 5* (1952): 157-73.

Bates, B. "Physician and Nurse Practitioner: Conflict and Reward," *Annals of International Medicine, 83,* (1975): 702-706.

Bateson, G. *Steps to an Ecology of Mind.* New York: Ballantine, 1972.

Bell, D. *The Cultural Contradictions of Capitalism.* New York: Basic Books, 1976.

Bettman, O. L. *The Good Old Days—They Were Terrible!* New York: Random House, 1974.

Blackburn, T. R. "Sensuous-Intellectual Complementarity in Science," *Science, 172* (1971): 1003-1007.

Bliss, A. and Cohen, E. D. *The New Health Professionals.* Germantown, Md.: Aspen Systems Corp., 1977.

Bloomfield, G. *The World Automotive Industry.* London: David and Charles, 1978.

Boulding, K. E. *Ecodynamics: A New Theory of Societal Evolution.* Beverly Hills, Cal.: Sage, 1978.

Burck, C. G. "How G. M. Turned Itself Around," *Fortune,* (January 16, 1978): 86-100.

————. "What's Good For the World Should Be Good for G.M.," *Fortune,* (May 7, 1979): 125-135.

————. "How G.M. Stays Ahead," *Fortune,* (March 9, 1981): 48-56.

Burnip, R., Erickson, R., Barr, G., Shinefield, H. and Schoen, E. "Well Child Care by Pediatric Nurse Practitioners in a Large Group Practice," *American Journal of Diseased Children, 130* (1976): 51-55.

Burns, T. and Stalker, G. M. *The Management of Innovation.* London: Tavistock, 1962.

Bursic, E. S. "Problems of PAs and Medex From Their Own Perspective," in A. Bliss and E. D. Cohen (eds.), *The New Health Professionals.* Germantown, Md.: Aspen Systems Corp., 1977.

Bullough, B. "Barriers to the Nurse Practitioner Movement: Problems of a Woman in a Woman's Field," *International Journal of Health Services, 5* (1975): 225-233.

Campbell, D. T. "Variation and Selective Retention in Socio-Cultural Evolution," in H. R Barringer, G. I. Blanksteen and R. W. Mack (eds.), *Social Change in Developing Areas.* Cambridge, Mass.: Schenkman Publishing Co., 1965.

————. "Evolutionary Epistemology," in P. A. Schlipp (ed.), *The Library of Living Philosophers—The Philosophy of Karl Popper.* Vol. 14, No. 1. LaSalle, Ill.: Open Court Publishing Co., 1974.

Campbell, J. P. "Contributions Research Can Make in Understanding Organizational Effectiveness," in S. L. Spray (ed.), *Organizational Effectiveness.* Kent, Oh.: Kent State University Press, 1976.

————. "On the Nature of Organizational Effectiveness," in P. S. Goodman and J. M. Pennings (eds.), *New Perspectives in Organizational Effectiveness.* San Francisco: Jossey-Bass, 1977.

————. Brownas, E. A., Peterson, N. G. and Dunnette, M. D. *The Measurement of Organizational Effectiveness: A Review of Relevant Research and Opinion.* San Diego: Naval Personnel Research Center, 1974.

Carnegie Commission on Higher Education. *Higher Education and the Nation's Health.* New York: McGraw-Hill, 1970.

Cavanagh, G. S. *American Business Values in Transition.* Englewood Cliffs, N.J.: Prentice-Hall, 1976.

Charney, E. and Kitzman, H. "The Child Health Nurse (Pediatric Nurse Practitioner) in Practice," *New England Journal of Medicine, 285* (1971): 1353-1358.

"Chrysler: A Whole New Ball Game," *Forbes,* (September 15, 1970): 25.

Churchman, C. W. *The Systems Approach.* New York: Delta, 1968.

Coleman, J. S. *Power and the Structure of Society.* New York: W. W. Norton, 1974.

Connolly, T. A., Conlon, E. J. and Deutsch, S. J. "Organizational Effectiveness: A Multiple Constituency Approach," *Academy of Management Review, 5* (1980): 211-218.

Davis, K. "Social Responsibility is Inevitable," *California Management Review, 19* (Fall, 1976): 14-20.

"Detroit's Uphill Battle," *Time,* (September 8, 1980): 46-52.

"Distress That Won't Go Away," *Business Week,* (January 12, 1981): 52-53.

Dixon, J. E. "Ask the Man Who Uses One—A Physician's Experience," *Physician's Associate, 2* (1972): 11-16.

Downs, A. *Inside Bureaucracy.* Boston: Little, Brown, and Co., 1967.

Drew, E. B. "The Politics of Auto Safety," *Atlantic Monthly, 218* (October, 1966): 95-102.

Drucker, P. F. *Concept of the Corporation.* New York: Mentor, 1972.

Dubin, R. "Organizational Effectiveness: Some Dilemmas of Perspective," in S. L. Spray (ed.), *Organizational Effectiveness.* Kent, Oh.: Kent State University Press, 1976.

Duncan, B., Smith, H. and Silver, H. "Comparison of Physical Assessment of Children by Pediatric Nurse Practitioners and Physicians," *Journal of Public Health, 61* (1971): 1170-1176.

Duncan, R. B. "Multiple Decision-Making Structures in Adapting to Environmental Uncertainty: The Impact on Organizational Effectiveness," *Human Relations, 26* (1973): 273-291.

Emery, J. C. *Organizational Planning and Control Systems: Theory and Technology.* London: Macmillan, 1969.

Etzioni, A. "Two Approaches to Organizational Analysis: A Critique and Suggestion," *Administrative Science Quarterly, 5* (1960): 257-278.

———. *Modern Organizations.* Englewood Cliffs, N.J.: Prentice-Hall, 1964.

Evan, W. M. "Organizational Theory and Organizational Effectiveness: An Exploratory Analysis," in S. L. Spray (ed.), *Organizational Effectiveness.* Kent, Oh.: Kent State University Press, 1976.

Fein, R. *The Doctor Shortage: An Economic Diagnosis.* Washington, D. C.: The Brookings Institution, 1967.

Fellers, R. J., Cohen, J. B., Tworek, R. K. and Campbell, E. I. *Attitudes of Illinois Physicians Towards the Hiring of Physicians Assistants.* Urbana, Ill.: University of Illinois, College of Medicine, 1976.

Fine, L. and Silver, H. "Comparative Diagnostic Abilities of Child Health Associate Interns and Practicing Pediatricians," *Journal of Pediatrics, 83* (1973): 332-335.

Finlay, R. "Decoding the Corporate Credibility Dilemma," *Business Quarterly,* (Summer, 1979): 43-55.

"Ford and the Future," *Dun's Review* (November, 1971): 27 + .

"Ford in the Future," *Forbes* (November 1, 1971): 24-25.

"Ford Shifts Gears to Stay in Race," *Detroit Free Press* (August 3, 1980): 1C.

"Ford's Hot Seat," *Wall Street Journal* (May 7, 1980); 1, 24.

Fottler, M. D. and Pinchoff, D. M. "Acceptance of the Nurse Practitioner: Attitudes of Health Care Administrators," *Inquiry, 13* (1976): 262-273.

Freeman, H. "The Present Status of Evaluation Research," in M. Guttentag (ed.), *Evaluation Studies Review Annual,* Vol. 2. New York: Sage Publications, 1977.

——— and Sherwood, C. C. *Social Research and Social Policy.* Englewood Cliffs, N.J.: Prentice-Hall, 1970.

⌡ Friedlander, F. and Pickle, H. "Components of Effectiveness in Small Organizations," *Administrative Science Quarterly, 13* (1967): 289-304.

Galbraith, J. *Designing Complex Organizations.* Reading, Mass.: Addison-Wesley, 1973.

Gaus, C., Morris, S. B. and Smith, D. B. "The Social Security Administration Physician Extender Reimbursement Study," in A. Bliss and E. D. Cohen (eds.), *The New Health Professionals.* Germantown, Md.: Aspen Systems Corp., 1977.

General Motors Corporation. "Comments by the General Motors Corporation to the Federal Energy Administration on Passenger Fuel Economy," (August, 1974).

————. *1974 General Motors Report on Programs of Public Interest,* 1975.

————. *1975 General Motors Report on Programs of Public Interest,* 1976.

————. *1980 General Motors Public Interest Report,* 1980.

⌄ Georgopoulos, B. S. and Tannenbaum, A. S. "A Study of Organizational Effectiveness," *American Sociological Review, 22* (1957): 534-540.

√ Ghorpade, J. *Assessment of Organizational Effectiveness.* Pacific Palisades, Cal.: Goodyear Publishing Co., 1971.

Golden, L. L. L. *Only By Public Consent.* New York: Hawthorne Books, 1968.

Gottesman, C. A. "World Auto Turmoil: The Maze," *Automotive Industries,* (July 1, 1975): 19-20.

Guzzardi, W. "Ford: The Road Ahead," *Fortune* (September 11, 1978): 37-48.

√ Hannan, M. T. and Freeman, Jr. "Obstacles to the Comparative Study of Organizational Effectiveness," in P. S. Goodman and J. M. Pennings (eds.), *New Perspectives on Organizational Effectiveness.* San Francisco: Jossey-Bass, 1977.

Henry, R. A. "Use of Physician's Assistants in Gilchrist County, Florida," *The PA Journal* (Summer, 1973): 25-29.

————. "Evaluation of Physician's Assistants in Gilchrist County, Florida," *Public Health Reports, 89* (1974): 232-249

"Henry Ford Is Still The Boss," *Automotive News,* (May 23, 1977): 6+.

Hickson, D. J., Hinnings, C. R., Lee, C. A., Schneck, R. E., and Pennings, J. M. "A Strategic Contingencies' Theory of Interorganizational Power," *Administrative Science Quarterly, 16* (1971): 216-229.

Hirschman, A. O. *Exit, Voice and Loyalty.* Cambridge, Mass.: Harvard University Press, 1972.

Hitt, M. A. and Middlemist, R. D. "A Methodology to Develop Criteria and Criteria Weightings for Assessing Subunit Effectiveness in Organizations," *Academy of Management Journal, 22* (1979): 356-374.

House, E. R. "The Conscience of Educational Evaluation," *Teachers College Record, 73* (1972): 405-414.

————. *Evaluating With Validity.* Beverly Hills: Sage Publications, 1980.

Hrebiniak, L. G. *Complex Organizations.* St. Paul Minn.: West Publishing Company, 1978.

"Industry Changes Tied to Worldwide Character," *Automotive News,* (September 19, 1977): 6.

"Inside Japan: The New No. 1," *Automotive Industries,* (September, 1980): 75.

Kahn, L. and Wirth, P. "The Modification of Pediatrician Activity Following the Addition of a Pediatric Nurse Practitioner to the Ambulatory Care Setting: A Time and Motion Study," *Pediatrics, 55* (1975): 700-708.

Kalisch, B. J. and Kalisch, P. A. "An Analysis of Physician-Nurse Conflict," *Journal of Nursing Administration, 7* (1977): 51-57.

Katz, D. and Kahn, R. L. *The Social Psychology of Organizations.* New York: Wiley, 1966.

Keeley, M. "A Social Justice Approach to Organizational Evaluation," *Administrative Science Quarterly, 23* (1978): 272-292.

Kelly, G. A. "The Language of Hypothesis: Man's Psychological Instrument," *Journal of Individual Psychology, 20* (1964): 137-152.

Kilmann, R., Pondy, L., and Slevin, D. *The Management of Organizational Design.* New York: North Holland, 1976.

Kirk, R. *Snow.* Caldwell, N. J.: William Morrow and Co., 1978.

Kissam, P. C. "Physician's Assistant and Nurse Practitioner Laws for Expanded Medical Delegation," in A. Bliss and E. D. Cohen (eds.), *The New Health Professionals.* Germantown, Md.: Aspen Systems Corp., 1977.

Kissick, W. "Effective Utilization: The Critical Factor in Health Manpower," *American Journal of Public Health, 58* (1968): 23-29.

Kristol, I. "On Economic Education," *Wall Street Journal,* (February 18, 1976): 18.

Lakatos, I. "Falsification and the Methodology of Scientific Research Programmes," in I. Lakatos and A. Musgraves (eds.), *Criticism and the Growth of Knowledge.* London: Cambridge University Press, 1970.

Lawrence, D. M. and Callen, W. "The Demand for New Health Practitioners," in R. Kane (ed.), *New Health Practitioners.* Washington, D. C.: Government Printing Office, 1975.

Lawrence, P. R. and Lorsch, J. W. *Organization and Environment.* Cambridge, Mass.: Harvard University Press, 1967.

Lees, R. "Physician Time-Saving by Employment of Expanded Role Nurse in Family Practice," *Canadian Medical Association Journal, 108* (1973): 871-875.

Lettvin, J. Y., Manturana, H. R., McCulloch, W. S. and Pitts, W. "What the Frog's Eye Tells the Frog's Brain," in W. S. McCulloch (ed.), *Embodiments of the Mind.* Cambridge, Mass.: MIT Press, 1965.

Longstreth, B. and Rosenbloom, H. D. *Corporate Social Responsibility and the Ethical Investor.* New York: Praeger, 1973.

"Losing A Big Segment of the Market—Forever?" *Business Week,* (March 24, 1980): 78-88.

Mahoney, T. A. and Frost, P. "The Role of Technology in Models of Organizational Effectiveness," *Organizational Behavior and Human Performance, 11* (1974): 127-38.

Mahoney, T. A. and Weitzel, W. "Managerial Models of Organizational Effectiveness," *Administrative Science Quarterly, 14* (1969): 357-365.

March, J. G. and Olson, J. P. (eds.). *Ambiguity and Choice in Organizations.* Bergen, Norway: Universitetsforlaget, 1976.

Margolis, H. "The Politics of Auto Emissions," *The Public Interest, 49* (Fall, 1977): 3-21.

Meadows, D. "Ford Needs Better Ideas—Fast," *Fortune,* (June 16, 1980): 82-86.

Meadows, D. H., Meadows, D. L., Randers, J. and Behrens, W. *The Limits to Growth.* New York: Signet, 1972.

Merenstein, J., Wolfe, H. and Barker, K. "The Use of Nurse Practitioners in a General Practice," *Medical Care, 7* (1974): 445-452.

Miles, R. H. *Macro Organizational Behavior.* Santa Monica, Calif.: Goodyear Publishing Company, 1980.

Miles, R. H. and Cameron, K. *Coffin Nails and Corporate Strategies.* Englewood Cliffs, N.J.: Prentice-Hall, 1982.

Morris, S. B. "Third Party Payment for the Services of the Assistant to the Primary Care Physician," in A. Bliss and E. D. Cohen (eds.), *The New Health Professionals.* Germantown, Md.: Aspen System Corp., 1977.

Motor Vehicle Manufacturers Association. *World Motor Vehicle Data.* Detroit: Motor Vehicle Manufacturers Association of the U.S., Inc., 1980.

Mott, P. E. *The Characteristics of Effective Organizations.* New York: Harper and Row, 1972.

"Mulling It Over," *Wall Street Journal,* (December 4, 1980): 1, 18.

Neghandi, A. R. and Reimann, B. C. "Task Environment, Decentralization, and Organizational Effectiveness," *Human Relations, 26* (1973): 203-214.

Nelson, E. C., Jacobs, A. R. and Johnson, K. G. "Patients' Acceptance of Physician's Assistants," *Journal of the American Medical Association, 288* (1974): 63-67.

Nystrom, P. C. and Starbuck, W. H. (eds.). *Handbook of Organizational Design.* London: Oxford University Press, 1980.

Ornstein, R. E. *The Psychology of Consciousness.* San Francisco: W. H. Freeman and Co., 1972.

Osborn, R. N. and Hunt, J. G. "Environment and Organizational Effectiveness," *Administrative Science Quarterly, 19* (1974): 231-246.

Ozimek, D. *The Nurse Practitioner: The Current Situation and Implications for Curriculum Change.* New York: National League for Nursing, 1976.

Parsons, T. "A Sociological Approach to the Theory of Organizations," *Administrative Science Quarterly, 1* (1956): 63-85.

Pennings, J. M. and Goodman, P. S. "Toward a Workable Framework," in P. S. Goodman and J. M. Pennings (eds.), *New Perspectives on Organizational Effectiveness.* San Francisco: Jossey-Bass, 1977.

Perrow, C. "The Analysis of Goals in Complex Organizations," *American Sociological Review, 26* (1961): 854-866.

Pfeffer, J. and Salancik, G. R. "Organizational Decision Making as a Political Process: The Case of a University Budget," *Administrative Science Quarterly, 19* (1974): 135-151.

————. *The External Control of Organizations: A Resource Dependence Perspective.* New York: Harper and Row, 1978.

Pickle, H. and Friedlander, F. "Seven Societal Criteria of Organizational Success," *Personnel Psychology, 20* (1967): 165-178.

Pondy, L. R. "Two Faces of Evaluation," in H. R. Melton and D. J. H. Watson (eds.), *Interdisciplinary Dimensions of Accounting for Social Goals and Social Organizations.* Columbus, Oh.: Grid Publishing Co., 1977a.

————. "Effectiveness: A Thick Description," in P. S. Goodman and J. M. Pennings (eds.), *New Perspectives on Organizational Effectiveness.* San Francisco: Jossey-Bass, 1977b.

————, Jones, J. M. and Braun, J. A. "Utilization and Productivity of the Duke Physician's Associate," *Socio-Economic Planning Sciences, 7* (1973): 327-352.

————, and Mitroff, I. I. "Beyond Open Systems Models of Organization," in B. M. Staw and L. L. Cummings (eds.) *Research in Organizational Behavior.* Greenwich, Ct.: JAI Press, 1978.

Post, J. E. *Corporate Behavior and Social Change.* Reston, Virginia: Reston Publishing Co., 1978.

Price, J. L. "The Study of Organizational Effectiveness," *Sociological Quarterly, 13* (1972): 3-15.

Purcell, T. and Cavanagh, G. *Blacks in the Industrial World: Issues for the Manager.* New York: Free Press, 1972.

Quinn, J. B. "General Motors Corporation: The Downsizing Decision," Unpublished case study, Amos Tuck School, Dartmouth College, 1978.

Rawls, J. *A Theory of Justice.* Cambridge, Mass.: Balknop Press, 1971.

Rittel, H. W. J. and Weber, M. M. "Dilemmas in a General Theory of Planning," *Policy Sciences, 4* (1973): 155-169.

Rohrbaugh, J. and Quinn, R. "Evaluating the Performance of Public Organizations: A Method for Developing a Single Index," *Journal of Health and Human Resources Administration, 2* (1980): 343-354.

Rukeyser, W. S. "Detroit's Reluctant Ride to Smallsville," *Fortune,* (March, 1969): 110-168.

Sackett, D., Spitzer, W., Gent, M. and Roberts, R. "The Burlington Randomized Trial of the Nurse Practitioner: Outcomes of Patients," *Annals of Internal Medicine, 80* (1974): 137-142.

Salancik, G. and Pfeffer, Jr. "The Bases and Uses of Power in Organizational Decision Making: The Case of a University," *Administrative Science Quarterly, 19* (1974): 453-473.

Scriven, M. "Goal-Free Evaluation," in E. R. House (ed.), *School Evaluation: The Politics and Process.* Berkeley: McCutchan, 1973.

Schulman, J. and Wood, C. "Experience of a Nurse Practitioner in a General Medicine Clinic," *Journal of the American Medical Association, 219* (1972): 1453-1461.

Schumpeter, J. A. *Capitalism, Socialism and Democracy.* New York: Harper and Brother, 1942.

Shaw, B. L. "The New Man in Town: The PA, *RN,* (October, 1970): 33.

Schuyten, P. J. "Chrysler Goes For Broke," *Fortune,* (June 19, 1978): 54-58.

Simon, H. A. "On the Concept of Organizational Goal," *Administrative Science Quarterly, 9* (1964): 1-22.

——. *Administrative Behavior,* 3rd ed. New York: Free Press, 1976.

Spitzer, W. O., Sackett, D. L. and Sibley, J. C. "The Burlington Randomized Trial of the Nurse Practitioner," *New England Journal of Medicine, 290* (1974): 251-256.

Spray, S. L. "Organizational Effectiveness: The Problems of Relevance," in S. L. Spray (ed.), *Organizational Effectiveness.* Kent, Oh.: Kent State University Press, 1976.

Stake, R. E. "The Countenance of Educational Evaluation," *Teachers College Record, 68* (1967): 532-540.

——. "To Evaluate an Arts Program," in R. E. Stake (ed.), *Evaluating the Arts in Education.* Columbus, Oh.: Merrill Publishing Co., 1975.

Starbuck, W. H. "Organizations and Their Environments," in M. Dunnette (ed.), *Handbook of Industrial and Organizational Psychology.* Chicago: Rand McNally, 1976.

√ Steers, R. N. "Problems in the Measurement of Organizational Effectiveness," *Administrative Science Quarterly, 20* (1975): 546-558.

√ ——. *Organizational Effectiveness: A Behavioral View.* Santa Monica: Goodyear Publishing Co., 1977.

Stein, G. "The Use of a Nurse Practitioner in the Management of Diabetes Mellitus," *Medical Care, 12* (1974): 885-890.

Stewart, J. H. "Factors Accounting for Goal Effectiveness: A Longitudinal Study," in S. L. Spray (ed.), *Organizational Effectiveness.* Kent, Oh.: Kent State University Press, 1976.

Suchman, E. A. *Evaluative Research.* New York: Russell Sage Foundation, 1967.

Sultz, H. A., Henry, O. M. and Carroll, H. D. "Nurse Practitioners: An Overview of Nurses in the Expanded Role," in A. Bliss and E. D. Cohen (eds.), *The New Health Professionals.* Germantown, Md.: Aspen Systems Corp., 1977.

"The Auto Clash Goes Global," *Dun's Review,* (April, 1978): 48-53.

Thompson, J. D. *Organizations in Action.* New York: McGraw-Hill, 1967.

—— and McEwen, W. J. "Organizational Goals and Environment," *American Sociological Review, 23* (1958): 23-30.

"To A Global Car," *Business Week,* (November 20, 1978): 102-113.

Todd, M. "The Physician's View," in D. M. Pitcairn and D. Flahault (eds.), *The Medical Assistant: An Intermediate Level of Health Care Personnel.* Geneva: World Health Organization, 1974.

Turner, I., Christian, J., Clemmings, L., Lashof, J., Noble, B., Omori, N., Shannon, I. and Strokosch, G. "The Evaluation of the Nurse Associate in a Variety of Health Care Settings." Presented at the American Public Health Association Meetings, Orlando, Florida, November, 1973.

Turner, I. and Zammuto, R. F. "Impact of the Pediatric Nurse Associate in the Health Care Delivery Process," *Pediatric Digest, 17* (1975): 29-37.

United States Energy Information Administration. *Monthly Energy Review,* (January, 1980).

————. *Monthly Energy Review.* (July, 1976).

United States General Accounting Office. *Progress and Problems in Training and Use of Assistants to Primary Care Physicians.* Washington, D. C.: General Accounting Office, 1975.

United States Public Health Service. *Physicians for a Growing America.* Washington, D. C.: U.S. Government Printing Office, 1959.

Vanderwicken, P. "What's Really Wrong at Chrysler," *Fortune,* (May, 1975): 176+.

Vickers, G. *The Art of Judgment.* New York: Basic Books, 1965.

————. *Value Systems and Social Processes.* New York: Basic Books, 1968.

Walker, C. T. H. *The Construction of the World in Terms of Fact and Value.* Oxford: B. H. Blackwell, 1919.

Walton, J. "A Methodology for the Comparative Study of Power: Some Conceptual and Procedural Applications," *Social Science Quarterly, 52* (1971): 39-60.

Ward's. *Automotive Yearbook.* Detroit; Ward's Reports, Inc., 1948.

————. *Automotive Yearbook.* Detroit: Ward's Communications, Inc., 1974.

————. *Automotive Yearbook.* Detroit: Ward's Communications, Inc., 1978.

Webb, R. J. "Organizational Effectiveness and the Voluntary Organization," *Academy of Management Journal, 14* (1974): 663-677.

Weick, K. E. *The Social Psychology of Organizing.* Second Edition. Reading, Mass.: Addison-Wesley, 1979.

————. "Re-Punctuating the Problem," in P. S. Goodman and J. M. Pennings (eds.), *New Perspectives on Organizational Effectiveness.* San Francisco: Jossey-Bass, 1977.

Weiss, C. H. "The Politicalization of Evaluation Research," *Journal of Social Issues, 26* (1970): 57-68.

Weiss, E. A. "The Future Opinion of Business," *Management Review,* (March, 1978): 8-15.

Weiss, R. S. and Rein, M. "The Evaluation of Broad-Aim Programs: A Cautionary Case and a Moral," *The Annals of the American Academy of Political and Social Sciences, 385* (1969): 133-145.

"What's Wrong At Chrysler? *Forbes,* (December 1, 1973): 28-33.

Williams, E. "Implications of Viewing Educational Evaluation as Research in the Social Sciences," in P. A. Taylor and D. M. Crowley (eds.), *Readings in Curriculum Evaluation.* Dubuque, Iowa: William C. Brown Co., 1972.

Wirth, P., Storm, E. and Kahn, L. "An Analysis of the Fifty Graduates of the Washington University Pediatric Nurse Practitioner Program," *Nurse Practitioner* (July-August, 1977): 18-23.

Wright, J. P. *On A Clear Day You Can See General Motors.* Grosse Pointe, Michigan: Wright Enterprises, 1979.

Yuchtman, E. and Seashore, S. E. "A System Resource Approach to Organizational Effectiveness," *American Sociological Review, 32* (1967): 891-903.

Zammuto, R. F., Turner, I. R., Miller, S., Shannon, I. R. and Christian, J. "The Effects of Clinical Settings on the Utilization of Nurse Practitioners," *Nursing Research, 28* (1979): 98-102.

Subject Index

Boldface numbers refer to figures and tables.

Author Index